Dedi

I dedicate this book to my parents, Elsie and Alfred Coombs, in recognition and gratitude for their patience, love and support and for understanding the impetuosity of youth. I truly believe that it was the Christian values taught to me as a child that opened my mind and heart to the poor young souls that I have tried to help. Also the parents. Their world is turned upside down as they struggle to come to terms with the terrible news that their child has a serious illness. I would also like to extend my gratitude to all the people who have worked alongside me over the years and have helped children in need and their parents. Lifting the dark clouds to allow an occasional bursts of sunshine into their lives is a wonderful feeling. There are many thousands of charity workers around the country who will know exactly what that means to them.

In looking back on my happiest childhood memories, I would like to extend my most sincere good wishes to Steven Furlong's family. Steven was my first 'best friend'. We never stopped laughing and everything seemed to be an adventure. Living and working down in Kent, I lost touch for many years and I was devastated to hear of his illness and passing at such a young age. I will never forget his wonderful smile that seemed to make the room light up. God bless you Steven.

Barry Coombs

On My Life

by
David J Colane

Printed & Bound in Great Britain by Clays Ltd
St Ives plc

Cover by Rob Francis www.ink-corporated.co.uk

Cover illustrations by Jake Ashpole

ISBN-13 978-0-9933295-2-4

PEN
SKILLS
PUBLISHING

Prologue

Is Christmas a time for giving? Yes I can confirm that. On 16th December 1992 two guys walked into my shop holding guns. One pointed at me, the other at one of my customers. The spokesman for the robbers shouted, 'give us the fucking money or he gets it.' I'd never seen guns before and was wondering if they were real. My daydreaming was interrupted by the sound of a gun being cocked. It was pressed against the head of the trembling old age pensioner. His eyes were like saucers as he nodded vigorously. I gave them the contents of the till. Merry Christmas!

During the process of dictating this story, it seemed at times as though I was referring to someone else's life. The memories were neatly stored in my cerebral archives and I smiled a hundred smiles as I drew them to the surface one by one. But there were moments when my bum twitched at the thought, 'did I really do that?'

The 1960's and 70's were incredible periods in history. It's as if fifteen years after the war had ended, the world decided to let its hair down and go mad for a while. I hope that you will be sympathetic and understanding when you read the early chapters of this book. Most of the sympathy should be directed towards my late parents. They truly had the patience of saints. I believe they understood me better than I understood myself.

David Colane said, 'people will laugh when they read this.' I said, 'what about the bits where I was crapping my pants with fear? He said, 'yeah, especially those bits!' I laughed and said, 'I expect loads of people did the things I did when they was young.' He rubbed his chin and looked at me. He sniffed and shook his head and replied, 'no, I don't think so, I think you'll find that you're very different!'

Maybe he's right, maybe I am different. I mean, I was very small when I was young! If you can understand why I did some of these crazy things then you're probably a better man than me Gungadin!

Today, I am proud of the certificates and pictures that adorn my walls at home. Memories of wonderful people and reminders of so many special events. But a few years ago there were a few people who thought that **I** should be certified. I think if I had been an observer at the time....I would have been one of them!

Choosing a title for the book was difficult. My original idea was 'Barry the Bookie' Then my two ex wives suggested, Barry the Bastard', whilst the lads at William Hill suggested 'Barry the Charity'. Colane wasn't very helpful. As I walked out of his office he called out, 'if I was you I would change my name to Alice, and emigrate.'

Get ready to use your imagination as I claw back the years. Read my story, warts and all and see what **you** think. On my life.....boring it isn't!.

Barry Coombs

4

Chapter one: Foetus recall

I was delivered into this world, on August 5th 1952, courtesy of the Salvation Army Mothers' Home in Clapton, East London. I was the youngest of four brothers and had come as a complete surprise to my parents. Especially my mother, who thought she had indigestion and went to the doctor expecting Milk of Magnesia.

My first recollection of sound was the word 'push' which was quickly followed by my first experience of physical abuse as someone grabbed me by the neck and started pulling.

I had been warm and comfortable for nine months, well fed and putting on weight at what seemed to be the 'acceptable rate'. But I was rapidly outgrowing my present habitat, hearing laughter and feeling various objects being placed on me, which I found quite objectionable! It caused me to hope that something better was waiting at the next stage, whatever that was to be. I will admit that I had no idea what I was expected to do with the objects but I've had a phobia about jugglers and performing seals ever since!

I can still recall the umbilical cord being severed and the feeling of exhilaration at being triumphantly raised towards the ceiling and seeing my first job opportunity. 'Jesus wants you for a sunbeam.' Oh! does he.....how much an hour? This was rapidly followed by my first experience of 'masochism' and 'injustice' as I was smacked on the arse and then cuddled by the perpetrator!

'There...there......... never mind........coochi cooo!' My arse was stinging! Never mind?...never bloody mind?? I glanced up preparing to speak my first words, it was then that I saw the invitation across her hat. 'Come and Join Us'. I pushed away with my feet. 'No thank you........ you must be having a laugh! Could you please put me back where I was.' Yes, it was lonely, but I was happy, safe from brutality and life was less complicated.

All to no avail I'm afraid! I was now being tightly wrapped in some sort of straight jacket material, with just my head protruding from one end. I now knew what claustrophobia was....whoopee!

Hi, I'm Barry Coombs. During my 35 years in the betting industry, I was often referred to as Barry the Bookie, by the winners that is........and sometimes Barry the bastard by the losers, as if I'd had some influence on the result! But at that moment in time I was Barry the baby. Being born! What a performance, I expect you all remember it.

With my arms pinned down by my sides and being lashed up in white swaddling cloth, I resembled a giant maggot........! What is a swaddling by the way?

I was taken to the family home in Northbank Road Walthamstow. A three bedroomed end of terrace overlooking a small easy to maintain garden laid to concrete, with a conservatory and a side entrance. As we walked into the entrance hall I glanced into my first mirror. Bloody hell I was receding and going bald! I hoped my mother was going to do something about this. I was given a conducted tour and eventually installed in the 'master suite.' I had a detached cot overlooking a Victorian commode laid to lino with an easy to maintain rug.

I was introduced to my eight year old brother, David. It was easy to see how impressed he was when he turned and pointed his catapult at me. That was my first official experience of having a weapon shoved in my face. Little did I know that this was the first of many such experiences that life had in store for me! I immediately wet my nappy. It transpired over the years that this was the most appropriate response to being threatened with a catapult. Now, a Smith & Weston 38 calibre on the other hand, normally induces a far messier body reaction. Especially, if all you are holding is a ball point pen.

'Would you like to hold your new baby brother?' asked mum, meaning well.

David reluctantly put down the catapult he was repairing and held out his arms.

As mum gently lowered me onto his lap, the expression on his face changed. 'He's all wet,' he shouted as he shoved me back towards mother. There was a smile on my face, 'so would you be if you'd just piddled your pants!' But that was nothing compared with what was on its way a minute later.

It was whilst being lowered onto David, that I got my first smell of bubble gum. It was an aroma that I would be smelling for many years to come.

Available in different flavours and colours, along with chewing gum, it represented the best value for money sweet that David could possibly invest in. He loved all sweets! Gobstoppers, liquorice, barley sugar, lollipops, you name it, he'd suck it. But chewing gum and bubblegum lasted forever. It would always make me smile when dad told him to take it out of his mouth whilst up at the food table. Defiantly, David would blow one last enormous bubble and pop it with his fork, before taking it out and putting it on the side of his plate. If there was a five minute break between dinner and afters, in would go the bubblegum again. He would keep it under his pillow at night so that nobody could pinch it! Chewing gum became dad's worst nightmare! It was impossible to get off the floor, especially from an easy to maintain garden laid to concrete.

I loved my new home! There was far more space than I had been used to during the previous nine months, and it was much brighter. Mum was one of fourteen children and dad was one of eight. You can imagine how many aunties, uncles and cousins I had!

Obviously, at that time I wasn't aware of a place called Piccadilly Circus, but as the days rolled on I began to think that the rest of civilisation was camped on our doorstep and had instant access to our door bell and knocker. Every time I nodded off, I was awoken by someone telling me how beautiful I was, and how I had my dad's eyes, my mum's nose and uncle Nobbie's smile. Thank goodness my legs and arms were my own, so I could push people away.

Sadly, this is exactly what I was doing at meal times!

No matter how often my mother insisted that it was good for me, the sight of that giant floppy milk pudding bearing down filled me with dread. Once it was compressed onto my face, the choice was simple.....suck it or suffocate!

It was sweet, it was sticky, it was on my face, in my hair, it was everywhere except where it should be.

'I can't make this out at all,' said mother. 'David had a full set of teeth and had to be beaten off with a stick before he ceased being breast fed.'

Well that's as maybe, but I hated the stuff! I would gag....be sick.....push and struggle. It became a battle of wits, with tears of resentment on my part and despair on my mother's.

Of course pushing it away wasn't helping. The more I pushed, the faster it came out. Oh! and as for being spoon fed from a bowl...... forget it. I was now managing to get my feet above my high chair table. As I slammed my feet down, my food bowl plus contents was being catapulted up into the air! It was up the curtains ....up the walls....up my mum. It was now so bad that my usual Mickey Mouse bib had been replaced by a bath towel.

Even when I did manage to take in the odd mouth full, I was throwing it up again a couple of minutes later. This fiasco could not be allowed to continue any longer. I couldn't eat.....mum couldn't sleep and David couldn't stop laughing. The only person putting on weight was the family dog.......it was gobbling up everything that hit the floor.

I was putting on no weight at all and meal times had become a fight to the death. After various tests by doctors and hospital staff, it was discovered that I had an internal disorder which was causing me to be sick. No! Surely not!!

I was quickly dispatched to a specialised unit in Tunbridge Wells, Kent. Various tubes and drips were set up and tests were carried out to find out what was wrong with me. One trainee nurse, upon seeing me laying there all wired and tubed up, suggested.

'Maybe he's just not hungry!'

It was an arduous hour and a half journey from North London to the hospital. No M25 in those days. My eldest brother, Donald, was the only driver in the family and he was away doing his National Service at the time. David offered to drive, but he was only eight years old and couldn't see over the dash board or reach the pedals.

It was a harrowing period for my parents. They had already lost their eldest son, Lawrence, two years after the war had ended. 16 year old Lawrence had been run down after a car being driven by a drunken vicar had mounted the kerb. The vicar had the audacity to knock on our door a week later and tell my father that it would have been God's will. As my father stepped forward, the sanctimonious bastard turned and ran. My father would have gone to prison if he'd caught him.

Apparently, my internal problems caused serious concern at one stage and I was in Tunbridge Wells for several weeks. Thankfully, the experts managed to sort it all out and I started putting on weight. I was allowed home again and found to my delight that in my absence the big floppy milk puddings had dried up. I was put on National Dried, which I managed to keep down.

As time went by, although I was very small in stature, everything else seemed to be developing at the right speed including my awareness and speech. However, my father did have cause to question that on one occasion.

Arriving home from work one evening, he found me sitting in my high chair finishing off a portion of rice pudding. He asked me the same question as usual, 'have you learned any new words today, Barry? ' I had mastered cat, dog, mum and dad and very proudly I sat up in my chair and said, 'Ah flobalob.' Dad stopped and thought for a few seconds. 'What was that again son?' I patiently repeated, a bit louder this time, 'Ah flobalob.' Dad turned and walked towards the doorway into the kitchen, scratching his head. He then turned and looked at me again just before opening the door, 'Ah flobalob,' he muttered.

Mum was dishing up dinner as he enquired, 'what does 'ah flobalob' mean, Else?'

Mum turned and smiled, 'he's been watching Bill and Ben the Flowerpot men on television and he's copying what they've been saying. It doesn't mean anything at all really.'

As he picked up his plate and started walking towards the dining room, my father was still muttering away to himself.......'a word that doesn't mean anything?' He turned to mother as they sat down at the table. 'Would you do me a favour? When 'ah flobalob' comes on again, have a quick look at what's on the other side would you?.......... anything in English will do!'

Now I loved seafood as a child and still do. Strange isn't it, I wouldn't drink mother's milk, so pure and clean but give me something that's been crawling around on the bottom of the ocean for two years and I'd fight you for it.

My mum was the youngest of fourteen children. Her brothers, 'the Charles's boys' were notorious. Three were bricklayers, two were plasterers three had stalls down Walthamstow market before it turned into Bangladesh. One, 'Honest Sid Charles' had a bookmakers pitch over Walthamstow Dog Stadium, and one, Percy Charles, had a sea food round in Walthamstow and South Chingford for over forty five years.

Sunday tea in our house used to consist of a few winkles and shrimps, cockles and mussels, a couple of whelks and if dad had a good week, a few prawns. I wasn't allowed winkles on account of how I was too small. One Sunday afternoon when dad wasn't watching, I snatched one off his plate and shoved it, shell included, into my mouth. Father looked round, 'Ullo!, I'm a winkle short'. (You didn't get many and he was good at maths). At that point I started coughing and spluttering!

The winkle was stuck in my throat. Quick as a flash I was turned upside down and thumped on the back. Out shot dad's winkle and I started to cry. As he reduced my crying to a whimper, there was a ring on the doorbell. In walked my father's posh sister, Ethel and her even posher husband, Leonard Penhallow.

Now Leonard Penhallow was the very top man at Kings Cross and Euston Stations. He was the person who used to greet the queen wearing top hat and tails, (that's Len not the Queen), as she got off a train. Leonard would have to bow and offer his arm as he escorted her to a waiting limousine. These days Her Majesty takes her chances with the rest of us. She is more likely to be greeted by some foreign vagrant offering her a copy of the Big Issue and told, 'that's a pound luv!'

As auntie Ethel and uncle Len walked into the dining room, I was still whimpering away, with the occasional sob thrown in. 'Hello darling,' said auntie, with a compassionate look on her face. 'Why are you crying, sweetheart?'

I looked at her and sobbed, 'I got d..d..daddy's w..winkle stuck d..down my throat.'

Auntie Ethel staggered backwards and looked at my mum, 'what did he just say?'

I was coming up to four years of age when we moved out of Walthamstow and into South Chingford. Three bed semi overlooking south facing garden laid to lawn with rear entrance and a garage. This was considered a move in the right direction in those days. But you had to go a little bit further north to have really made it. You had to be 'over the hill' into the Ridgeway area.

The hill in question was Chingford Mount, (Mount being short for Mountain I believe!) which is a one in six gradient. That probably means very little to anyone who hasn't tried to ride a bike up it! On a hot summer's day you would be well and truly f..... well you had to be bloody fit that's for sure. Coming down however was very different! It was tantamount to taking on the giant slalom at Grenoble!

Brother David had pestered the life out of mum and dad to buy him a racing bike. My father had picked up a first dividend on Littlewoods pools a year earlier and we had all enjoyed a few special treats. It was with great trepidation that he bought David a Dawes Dalesman for his fourteenth birthday. It had drop handlebars a racing saddle, 9 speed Campagnolo gears and twin drinking bottles! What more could you ask for, absolutely wonderful technology....twin drinking bottles...wow! What more could you ask for indeed? Well, you could try asking the recipient to abide by the code of the road and to drive very carefully. You could try but you would probably be wasting your breath!

My eldest brother, Donald had finished his National Service and was back working for the family building business. Dad had purchased an ex army Standard Van which had a canvas back. It made a great tent.....when dad wasn't using it of course. Around 4.30 one afternoon, Donald was driving dad to see a well to do customer living in North Chingford. This was where the big money could be earned.

The sun was shining brightly that day and the van was slowly clawing its way up Chingford Mount in second gear. It had just reached the halfway point, when suddenly there was a flash of red white and blue and David nearly took off as he came hurtling over the top of the hill.......with his arms folded.....chewing gum.   With their combined speeds, he went past dad at around 50mph and they exchanged glances. Donald shoved his hand in his mouth to suppress the urge to laugh. Dad had not found it amusing. When they arrived home an hour later, David had already locked his bike in the garage and put the key back on the hook. He knew what was coming. When dad told mum what he had seen she nearly passed out. David was grounded for a fortnight. As mum popped in to say goodnight to him a little later on, she said, 'you do worry me sometimes.' I was due to hear these words a few times during the oncoming years.

Chapter two: My first best friend

I started my education at Chase Lane primary school, although my size was still more suitable for a nursery. I befriended Steven Furlong who lived opposite me and was the same age. The Furlong family was large in number and they all worked very hard. They built up one of the largest roofing companies in the country and then went into housing development. Today, thousands of people live in homes built by the Furlong family over the years, through one of their many subsidiaries.

I used to go into Steven's house after school and sometimes we would play hide and seek. On one occasion I had climbed with great difficulty, into the airing cupboard and curled up in a ball. Steven was supposed to be counting to a hundred before coming to find me. However, unbeknown to me, Steven's mum and dad had come home early and had bought him an ice lolly. As he sat and ate it in the kitchen, he totally forgot all about me. Nobody else knew I was in the house. After a quarter of an hour had passed, I was feeling very pleased with myself to think that he was having such trouble finding me. Suddenly, I heard someone coming up the stairs and as the airing cupboard door was opened I sprung out roaring like a lion. 'Aaaaargh!!' Mrs Furlong staggered backwards and screamed. As I ran down the stairs, I passed Mr Furlong coming up two treads at a time. As I ran towards the back door, Steven

16

jumped up and ran with me. We were halfway up York road before we stopped to get our breath back.

'What are we running for....what was that scream?', gasped Steven.

I explained what had happened and said, 'maybe I should go back and apologise for making her jump.'

Steven said that although it was a nice gesture, it would probably be for the best if I wasn't there when she got back on her feet.

I received a ban from the house until the dust had settled, but Mrs Furlong laughed about it eventually, about a year later.

Several of the boys went on to achieve success in amateur boxing. David Furlong was the Southern Area Welterweight champion and Tony was a finalist in the ABA championships.

Their sister Joan used to babysit me, David and our sister Carol on a Friday or Saturday night whilst mum and dad went out for a drink with their brothers and sisters. One year, Joan came on holiday with us to Clacton on Sea. To this day, Joan remembers that holiday with great affection. Being one of sixteen children in the late 1950s was hard. Money in those days didn't stretch much beyond feeding, clothing and paying the bills. Joan said that she was so excited because it was her first real holiday. My mum and dad used to say what a lovely girl Joan was. She always said thank you and was a pleasure to have around. But, as mentioned, my mum and dad were no strangers to large families, mum being the youngest of fourteen children and dad was one of eight. So they knew what it was like to have to go without sometimes.

Steven Furlong was a lovely lad. We were both the youngest in our families and would spend hours over the park together. We laughed at everything.

When he left school, Steven worked hard and went on to establish a successful roofing and building business. He had a beautiful house overlooking the park and was happily married with children when tragedy suddenly struck. He was diagnosed with Motor Neurone Disease. Steven came from a family of fighters but sadly this was one fight that he was destined to lose. At the age of 48 he passed away. He was my very first, 'best friend' and I am proud to have known him.

I can still picture my mum and Mrs Furlong standing, chatting away, swapping stories at the garden gate. I often smile at the thought of the hide and seek games. I doubt if there are many seven year olds who could climb up into an airing cupboard, curl up in a ball, and stay there for a quarter of an hour. Come to think of it.......I must have looked a right idiot sitting there.

I was almost nine years old when we moved again, down to Margate this time. Nine bedroom detached overlooking large south facing garden, laid to lawn with four chalets.

No! There hadn't been a population explosion. Mum and dad had finally got round to buying the seaside guest house they....mum.....had always wanted.

Dad wanted to emigrate to Southern Rhodesia. His ex partner Charlie Miller was doing very well out there and often wrote to dad, but mum getting pregnant with me had put the kybosh on that. Just think, I could have been born in Rhodesia. Mind you they would have had a bloody long way to travel and see me in Tunbridge Wells every week.

I started at St John's School, Margate and found that I had inherited a love for music. My father was a good pianist and mother had a fine soprano voice. So with toes tapping and music in my soul I joined the St John's School silver band.

My musical experience up to that point had revolved around learning the recorder.

My band leader was impressed when I passed this information onto him and he sat spellbound as I quickly knocked out my renditions of Ba Ba Black Sheep and London's Burning. Imagine my surprise therefore, when he opened the store cupboard and gave me a gigantic Tuba, along with a few words of encouragement. 'See how you get on with that lad.' I was still very small and the Tuba seemed very big. Thankfully, one of the teachers saw me dragging it across the netball pitch and very kindly gave me a lift home.

My father was down at the library changing his book at the time. Upon arriving home he enquired as to my whereabouts. Mother informed him that I was in the guest lounge. Dad peered round the door and saw a Tuba on the armchair, with a pair of legs sticking out the bottom. Resisting the temptation to laugh, he strolled over and looked behind the large, shiny instrument.

I had been sitting there for fifteen minutes and had lost all feeling in my legs. 'Hello dad, it's a tuba,' I groaned. Encouragingly he said, 'come on then, give us a tune.'

I never bothered with pressing down any of the valves. I just held on tight with both hands, took a deep breath and as the front of my face disappeared into the mouthpiece I started spitting and blowing for all I was worth, Spprreeew...Spreoooow....Sprraargh. After thirty seconds, my toes had curled up, I'd gone bright red and all the wax had shot out of my ears. Dad put his hand up to his face but I could see he was laughing. 'Dinner's on the table son,' he said and turned to walk away. 'Dad!.....dad!...' I called, as he reached the door and turned to face me. 'Could you lift it off me please!'

With the benefit of hindsight, the band leader asked me what instrument I would like to play. I quite liked the look of a French horn, but my French wasn't that good , so I settled for the Tenor horn. There was no holding me back now and I went on to perform many concerts for charity with the school band. Also, I was once part of a large amalgamation of school brass bands that performed down in Plymouth. It was conducted by none other than Sir Malcolm Sergeant himself. I stayed with the band for another five years.

During the later part of this period, my brother, David was touring the world singing in a rock band. I could read and write music now, but despite my pleas he was adamant that they did not need a tenor horn player!

One of the nicest aspects of playing in the school silver band was that we would often entertain the residents of old people's homes, or 'Care Homes' as they are now called. The only difference being the exorbitant prices charged today! I met some grand old characters on my travels and I can still remember some of their stories, related to me over a cup of tea or a glass of Sanatogen tonic wine.

Many told me about the war and how it had affected them. Some had lost members of their family and had endured tremendous hardship. One lovely old lady told me that soon after she had been evacuated out of London, her house had been bombed. One year later she received news that her husband had been killed in action. She had lost absolutely everything, yet she told me several funny stories about her life after the war and how she had learned to live with the heartbreak of starting all over again. I was fifteen years old and felt so humble in the presence of such a brave and lovely person.

I was very happy and contented during that period of my life and I made a promise to myself. One day I would try to do something to help those less fortunate. My motto became. 'There but for fortune go I.'

Little did I know at that time how many wonderful, brave and caring people I would meet during the oncoming years. Even today, it never ceases to impress me that so many people are prepared to dedicate their whole life to caring for others. I consider it a privilege to have been able to help just a few of those many good causes, especially those concerning children. We haven't quite reached that part of my story yet because for the next few years I was to become Barry the rebel.

Refusing to be labelled or typecast and inspired by the adventures of Robert Louis Stevenson, I was convinced that something special was waiting for me out there! As to where and what it was, I didn't have a clue. I figured that I would recognise it when I found it......or **it found me!**

I have looked back in total horror at the next period of my life and have to consider the possibility that somewhere along the genetic line there had been a lunatic in the family.

It was as if I had taken a look at my prospects and decided that life was going to be too easy. What could I do to screw it up? What would it be like to struggle?..........to know hardship and pain? Well I was certainly going to be finding out!

My bum still twitches today, when I consider the many different outcomes that could have prevailed in some of my escapades. It was as if I had thrown down the gauntlet and challenged my destiny.

Chapter three: My first car

I completed my education by attending art college for two years. I loved art and technical drawing and had decided that I wanted to be an architect. I took up employment as a junior draughtsman/designer with Bostocks Builders.

I also had to learn estimation and quantity surveying as part of my overall career plan. My father had been a master builder for thirty years prior to buying the guest house. He was totally au fait with blue prints and standard building practice etc. He was very pleased with my chosen career and showed a great interest in my progress. He was always on tap to explain a symbol or terminology that I was either not familiar with or had forgotten.

I invested in driving lessons and longed for the time when, after dancing the night away at Dreamland Ballroom, I could say those magical words to a beautiful young lady. 'I've got my car outside. If we drive along to the North Foreland car park we can see the lighthouse.'

Brother David had often crawled indoors at seven in the morning with eyes like piss holes in the snow. He had a Morris Oxford saloon car complete with a sunroof. Along with his best mate, Les Trimmer, they had spent many a night with a couple of holiday makers of the female variety, parked in the total darkness of the North Foreland cliff top car park. No doubt they were discussing the history of the Isle of Thanet, the Viking invasions and describing the pain and anguish of a broken heart. 'Is it really possible for me to fall in love again, and 'would you like to sit on my lap and stick your head up through the sunroof?'

He doesn't embarrass easily but was caught on the hop on one occasion when he took a young lady home to meet mum and dad. They walked into the guest house just as dad was serving drinks in the lounge bar. The girl was a stunner who spoke very nicely and came from a well to do family. David had been on a big crusade blagging local talent for some time, so God knows what this, 'class act' was doing on his arm. In front of a house full of guests, he proudly announced, 'Mum and Dad, this is Lucy'. As Lucy held her hand out to shake, Mum suddenly blurted out, 'don't tell me.....Lucy Lastic!!' As the room erupted with laughter, David's jaw dropped and the girl stood there mortified. Mum was as bad as David at times.

Another occasion that brings a smile to my face was at breakfast one summer's morning. David was seventeen and I was ten We were eating in the family day room. Mum was in the kitchen dishing up breakfast and passing it through the serving hatch to my father who was waiting on guests in the dining room. We heard a ring at the doorbell and carried on eating our cornflakes. The next minute dad came marching in and looked down at us. 'David! There's a girl standing on the doorstep crying. Go and sort it out...NOW!' My brother was responsible for much of my teenage

24

education and had told me many exciting stories about the formation of the universe....the industrial revolution, the importance of being a responsible member of society. He also told me how great life was before some interfering bastard invented girls' tights. I really missed him when he joined the army later that year.

I passed my driving test and dad bought me a Singer Gazelle saloon car......with a sunroof! It was only when I read the owner's manual that I found out that David had been abusing the real reason for a car having a sunroof in the first place. I found it very difficult to get one leg out of it!

I had been the baby of the family and had benefitted from mum and dad being 'well established' by the time I came along. Central heating, hot running water, an indoor toilet and a bathroom. I took it all for granted. I never believed David's stories about candles, tin baths, and dad's Army coat on the bed in winter until years later when dad told me it was true.

There had been a proviso attached to dad buying me the car. I had to take him and mum out for a ride now and then. It was a small price to pay in return for driving around in such a beautiful car. Apart from anything else, dad would always generously fill up the petrol tank whenever we went out for the day. That would normally see me ok for the rest of the week. I suppose I should feel guilty at not having informed my father that the car was far more economical than he had come to believe.

He was a great dad to me and I always suspected that he knew the car did more than twenty miles to the gallon. There was always plenty of petrol left over at the end of a day's outing but he never questioned the high ratio of predictability that the fuel tank would always be nearly empty the next time he and mum wanted to go somewhere. The bottom line was, rightly or wrongly, he never asked so I never volunteered.

During my early driving years there was no such thing as a breathalyser! The drinking driving rules were basically advisory and co-operation from the public relied heavily on their application of common sense. Mind you, there were heavy fines for people who fell out of the car and headfirst onto the road if a police officer opened the car door, as my mate found out at 3am one Saturday. Also, if you were pulled up and suspected of being 'drunk in charge of a vehicle' the officer would tell you to leave the car where it was and pick it up the following day. This was a particular pain in the arse if you were twenty miles from home or halfway through the Blackwall Tunnel. The non existence of breathalysers was just as well really because I was now heavily dedicated to the amber nectar. Friday and Saturday night and Sunday lunchtime were my sacred AA periods! No, nothing to do with the Automobile Association or Alcoholics Anonymous. These periods were spent in the company of my fellow members of the Alcohol Appreciation Society. Our local group was known as 'The

Walking Dead'. We even ended up with our own little signature tune, written especially for us by David, who came out with us for a drink one night.

He had led the public bar into a little sing song medley with my mate Brian on the piano. Having advised us of the words earlier in the evening, he decided to release our new signature tune to the public, straight after he'd finished a rendition of that old chestnut, 'Auntie Mary Had A Canary Up The Leg Of Her Drawers'

He looked at us and nodded and we all sang along with the words to our new song. *__Here we are again me lads, they call us the walking dead. A pint of lager in each hand and throw one over me ead!__* *Andy Lloyd Webber watch out!*

I remember that night for another reason as well! David had given me the best bit of advice I'd had up to that point in my life. Several of my mates were glad of it as well. He told us of the night he'd taken out a local beauty queen for a meal and quite a few bevies. (In short, they were pissed). As he hammered it (the car that is) along the Margate to Broadstairs country road, he became aware of a flashing blue light trying to catch him up. A born survivor he said to Miss Ramsgate, 'quick hoist your skirt up and hang your knockers out yer blouse, (he was a smooth talking bastard).

As he pulled over, the police car pulled in behind and two officers stepped out. He wound down the window and said, 'good evening can I help you?'

Whilst one officer walked around the Morris Oxford admiring the stickers, one of which said 'support free love, see driver for details', his colleague had his note pad out. He looked into the car and said, 'good evening sir, is this your tits? David then explained to us, what a Freudian slip was. After he and his fellow officer had admired the view, the police officer let him drive on with a warning to 'be careful sir, don't be in such a hurry, take your time.' As David drove off, he smiled and said, 'I'm staying the night so I've got all the time in the world officer.' The weirdest thing was, I found myself praying that I would have the opportunity to put that particular exercise to the test one day!

My most embarrassing 'alcohol induced' moment came one evening when I drove home from the pub, three parts sozzled. It had been my mother's regular practice to open the wrought iron gates to the driveway before going to bed. Consequently, I had got used to the gates being open when arriving home. But one night, God Bless her, she forgot.

On a normal night I would probably have spotted that the gates were shut! But this had been a Friday night, enough said!

I hit the gates at what I considered to be a 'reasonable speed.' I heard a sound similar to machine gun fire as the gates bounced back and forth along both sides of the car. Courtesy of the dwarf walls on each side of the driveway, Due to my being distracted by the rata tat tat noise I neglected to apply my foot brake in time and demolished half of the entrance porch. I opened the car door and staggered through the bricks into the hallway. I was dying for a pee as my mother appeared in her dressing gown and slippers.

'What was that noise....what's happened?' she asked.

'Nothing to worry about mum,' I slurred, 'go back to bed, it's just a scratch!' At this point I wanted to believe it myself.

Mum walked over and looked through the patterned glass of the street door. She could see into the porch and spotted the front of the car poking through the wall.

As she walked back past me to go upstairs again, she said those immortal words. 'You do worry me sometimes Barry!'

The next morning I was up, washed, corn flaked and out of the house in double quick time My father hadn't appeared in the kitchen which I was quietly feeling grateful for, but unfortunately, I was soon to find out why. As I walked out into the driveway, there was my dad, picking up bricks and clearing the debris from around the car. I sheepishly got into the car and started the engine. I wound down the window and said, 'sorry dad!' Sadly, he just looked at the ground and slowly shook his head.

That was probably one of the saddest moments in my life. I felt a right bastard.

My father had been a sergeant in the army during the war. I had often asked him what it was like when he was in France and Germany, but he would never talk about it. I always considered that he was shielding me from the horrors of war. I remember asking him why it was that the TV companies kept showing the concentration camps. I found it very sad and depressing to think that people could ever treat fellow human beings in such an unforgivable way.

My father explained that sadly, human nature being what it was, if people were allowed to forget the horrors of war, they would begin to glorify it.

Dad only ever told me of one incident from his army days. Around the middle of 1944, he was shipped back to England and put in charge of a section of Italian prisoners being held in Dartmoor prison. One day, he was in charge of a work party clearing ditches or something, just outside the prison walls. Suddenly, a young lad made a run for it. As a guard raised his rifle my dad gave the order to hold his fire. A vehicle was dispatched and the lad was picked up and returned within the hour. When asked by the officer in charge of his section, why he had given the order, my father explained that they were in the middle of Dartmoor, there was nowhere to run. The officer concerned, unlike my father, had not been overseas and had not seen action. The officer implied that it was not the place of a sergeant to challenge standing orders which were, 'anyone attempting to escape would be shot'. My father replied, 'with respect sir, shooting an unarmed eighteen year old boy in the back, would make us no better than the Germans'. The young second lieutenant reported the incident to his commanding officer, who immediately agreed with my father. Dad had thought of his own two sons, Lawrence and Donald, who were evacuated down in Cornwall. This young lad was eighteen years old, he just wanted to go home.

I had to pay for the car to be repaired and re-sprayed and I bought my dad some of his favourite cigars. Luckily for me he was a good builder, otherwise I would have had to pay for repairing the brickwork.

Chapter four: The grey lady

Hands up those of you that have been ghost hunting and I don't mean sitting in a room with the light out! I'm talking about graveyards at three in the morning, wandering around the underground vaults of a derelict castle or finding yourself in the middle of a pitch black forest beside the 'dog pond' whilst waiting for the 'Monster of the Swamp' to appear!........everyday stuff really I suppose.

Here's the type of situation we are talking about, see if you can identify with this. Have you ever found yourself walking through an overgrown graveyard, alone in total darkness, with thick mist rising up from the ground, when suddenly an icy cold claw grabs you across the back of your neck? NO? Well neither have I.........fuck that!

However, I was a founder member of the 'KADPILDS'. Now there's no need to worry if you don't know what a KAD or a PILD is, because they are only the initials of a special organisation. They translate to the 'Kent Apparitions of Demonic Phantoms and Images of the Living Dead Society.' Brilliant isn't it? Have you any idea how much alcohol five pub regulars have to consume on a Friday night, in order to come up with a name like that?

Or, the state they must be in to even feel the need to come up with a name like that and all that it implies. Have a good stiff drink before reading on!

One of the foremen at Bostocks was a guy called Frank Arnison. Over a cup of tea one day, he told me that his mate had recently seen the ghost of the 'Grey Lady' at a place called Oxley Bottom. It was part of the Deal to Dover Rd, or conversely the Dover to Deal Rd............ depending on which way you were walking!

Later that day, I found myself in the public library, as you do, and I looked up the history of the area in question. Sure enough, the ghost of the Grey Lady did occasionally appear at Oxley Bottom and was normally seen during the period of a full moon. She was called the 'Grey Lady' by the way.....because she was grey!

I mentioned it to my mate, Ian Carden, and a few of the lads down at the Butlins bar near Margate. 'Why don't we get up a party and go looking for her?', I enthused, as we all walked into the public bar that evening. I could see from the expressions on their faces that it was probably something they wanted to think about........one day!

Initially, the info was about as welcome as a fart in a lift. It was 7 o'clock on a Friday night and we were all sober. I could tell that Ian was interested when he called along the bar, 'sounds a great idea Coombsy..........your round!

As the evening rolled on, the subject of ghosts cropped up again, when it was mentioned that there was once a public gallows, (did you ever hear of a private one?), situated at the crossroads on the D to D road and that there were rumours concerning the ghost of a famous highwayman called 'Big Dick'. He was called Big Dick by the way, because he was seven foot tall!....not what you were thinking.

As the bell rung for last orders, I was determined to create interest in the Grey Lady, so I casually tossed in the information that I had forgotten to mention earlier.....'she's got big knockers!' Before you could say 'poltergeist', we had a mini bus full.

On the evening of the very next full moon, bang on closing time, we commenced our journey into the unknown.

We had everything you needed for a ghost hunting expedition. Four crates of beer and forty bags of crisps! Plus, the official ghost hunters guide opened on page 3 'What To Do If You See A Ghost!' I remember it as a being a very thin book with the words *run* or *running* and lots of swearing in virtually every paragraph. Taking no chances, I had a crucifix round my neck, a clove of garlic in each pocket and a sharpened wooden stake at the ready.

At precisely 'something' past midnight, we arrived at Oxley Bottom, parked up and unloaded the provisions. We sampled a bottle of beer each to make sure that it hadn't gone off during the journey.

It was almost 'something' to one as we set off through the forest to try to find a derelict chapel that we had been told about.

I'm sorry to be so vague about the times, but unfortunately, during our journey, the big hand had dropped off my watch. I quickly looked into the ghost hunters guide to see if this was significant of anything evil or mysterious.

To my amazement, on page seven there was a relevant paragraph. 'If during the journey to your ghost hunting venue, you should happen to notice that the big hand on your watch has dropped off, turn to page fifteen. Oh my God! My hands were shaking and my heart was palpitating as I quickly turned to page fifteen.

Page fifteen was missing!

We wandered aimlessly through the undergrowth in total darkness. Various comments were being voiced as to our reasons for being there. As he watered a tree, John, who was a self confessed admirer of 'big knockers' claimed that he was going to 'give her one,' if she showed up. He quickly went off the idea when Ian pointed out that she was over three hundred years old.

Two 'ghostless' hours later, all the beer and crisp were gone. Ian turned to me and said. 'Don't look so worried Baz, what's the matter mate?' To his amazement I replied. 'I just can't stop worrying about my big hand, come on let's piss off'.

The first thing I did when I got home was to turn out the cupboard that the Ghost Hunters Guide had been in. There was page fifteen, wedged between the Beano album and a Playboy magazine. With baited breath I picked it up and turned it over and there was the answer I had been searching for. A full page advert. 'Timex Watches For All Occasions.'

We repeated our ghost hunting excursions on three consecutive full moons and drew a blank each time. It was suggested that we should give it one more try, but with a slight change in approach. A motion was put forward that we take six crates of beer and fifty bags of crisps. It was carried unanimously.

The chosen night turned out to be a Saturday and I got a phone call from Ian at nine thirty on the morning in question. 'We're not going to see any ghosts, Baz, he moaned.....I reckon she's bloody dead mate!' Before I had a chance to reply, he realised what he had said and rolled up. 'Yeah....she would be wouldn't she?' I had to admit that the idea was wearing a bit thin so I asked him what he had in mind and to my surprise he suggested, 'let's spice things up a bit.' I'll drive down there earlier in the evening and hide somewhere. I will be wearing white rags, whiten my face and darken my eyes to look like a skeleton...... with blood dripping out of my mouth.'

I told him I thought it was a brilliant idea, but suggested that he should not stop for petrol on the way.

We had three girls, including the pub barmaid, among the ten people on board that night. When we got to the parking area there was no sign of Ian's car, which was good because I realised that he might not have thought of that.

We made our way to the old chapel and got stuck into the beers and crisps. I was more nervous than the others at this point because I didn't know where or when   Ian was suddenly going to appear, or jump out.

It was one o'clock in the morning (new watch) when we heard something moving in the undergrowth. As we peered into the gloom, we became aware of a ghostly white shape in the distance. Suddenly a female voice amongst us moaned, oh fuck! At the sound of her voice, the ghostly apparition turned and looked in our direction. It suddenly let out a blood curdling high pitched scream and started running towards us through the bracken, growling and screaming and waving its arms.

Every one of us jumped up and hit the ground running. The girls were screaming and you could hear various puffing voices shouting 'oh fuck....oh fuck me.' It must have been a personal best time for the two hundred yards for all of us.

All ten of us came bursting out of the trees and undergrowth and ran towards the van. A courting couple had parked quite close to us and a naked bum was seen going up and down. As we stampeded towards their car, screaming and waving our arms in the air, two terrified faces appeared at the passenger side window. 'Run....quick run,' we shouted as the girl in the car started screaming.

As we piled into the mini bus, Ian suddenly came bursting out of the trees like a white banshee, and ran towards us waving his arms and screaming. There was blood running from his mouth and dripping onto his shroud.

The couple in the car were both screaming for help and I remember thinking, 'I bet that's dampened your ardour, mate.

We managed to shut the door just as Ian arrived. He commenced banging on the sides of the van and peering in through the windows. He looked so convincing that for one fleeting moment I considered the possibility that the reason Ian's car wasn't there was because Ian wasn't there! That would mean......I started screaming along with the others as I fumbled for the van keys.

There was the sound of an engine starting up but it wasn't ours. The couple in the car screeched away burning rubber. They were still stark bollock naked and she had mascara streaks over her face. I often wonder if they'd driven all the way home like that....or maybe got pulled over by the police for speeding and that same copper saying, 'Oh no, not again, this is getting bloody ridiculous! Just wait until I get my dick book out of my pocket!'

As I drove back towards Margate, everyone in the van was hysterically talking at once. 'That wasn't a grey haired old lady....that was a man,' said Brian.

'Maybe it was Big Dick,' said one of the girls.

It was all very convincing and I still wasn't certain that it had been Ian.

When we met at lunchtime the next day, the whole Butlins bar was buzzing with speculation as to who or what it was that we had seen in the woods the night before. I was looking forward to shaking hands with Ian and saying 'well done', but where was he? I had never known him to be late on a Sunday!

He was unusually late that day, and when he did appear, he looked washed out and tired.

Brian looked at him and scoffed, 'Cor! you missed all the fun last night mate. We got chased by this bloody phantom thing with blood all dripping down its face. It was trying to get into the van to kill us, wasn't it lads?'

Ian listened to them all and then, when he was convinced that they had all fallen for it, he announced, 'It was me lads and lasses..... I was the phantom thing.'

They all stopped talking and gazed at him in amazement! They didn't know whether to laugh or cry.

Suddenly, a voice muttered, 'you bastard,' I peed my pants because of you.'

I couldn't think of any other time that a girl....or anyone come to that, had stood up in a crowded pub and openly admitted to peeing their pants the night before, but Jill did, that day.

Ian sat at the bar and sipped his beer, he looked really rough, as though he hadn't had any sleep at all.

'Listen! I've got something to tell you all, you're not going to believe this!' Ian had gone white in the face.

After you had driven off, I started to walk back to my car. In order that you wouldn't suspect anything, I had driven to the other side of the forest and parked in a lay by. I had then made my way to the chapel from the opposite direction. The quickest way to the car now was to walk back the way you had run out and then past the chapel, about another half mile or so.

I was walking along, quietly laughing at you lot running and screaming, when suddenly, as I approached the derelict chapel, I began to feel very cold and the hair on the back of my neck was standing up. As I peered ahead I saw the ghostly apparition of an old lady. There was light shining from her eyes and she was slowly gliding towards me.....she had no feet! I stopped in my tracks but she kept on coming, she was now about fifty yards away and closing. Suddenly it wasn't funny anymore.

I turned round and started walking as quickly as possible back the way I came. I kept looking behind me but she was still following, if anything, she was gaining on me. I started to run and continued to look round every few seconds. She was still gaining on me and I could now see her face quite clearly. I was fascinated by the way she just seemed to be gliding along, about a foot off the ground.

I knew that I was nearing the car parking area and took one last glance over my shoulder to see how close she was.........she had gone!

I stopped running and stood there panting, staring into the gloom to see if I could spot her. Suddenly I heard a hissing noise followed by cackling, hysterical laughter. I suddenly felt as cold as ice and spun round.

There she was right in front of me, less than six feet away. Her eyes were shining brightly and her hands were stretched out in front of her. They were the hands of a skeleton. I had to move fast and realised my best bet was the car parking area. I put my head down and charged towards her. I felt her clothing brush against me as I seemed to pass through her. Within seconds I had broken through the bushes and into the car park and I continued to run towards the car park entrance.

I didn't stop running until I reached the main road and turned one last time to look behind me. She was standing by the bushes laughing and waving.

I felt something strange and looked down at my cloths. I was covered in thick cobwebs from head to foot and there were hundreds of spiders crawling over me.

It took me fifteen minutes to get rid of the spiders, they were in my hair and inside my clothing. It then took almost another hour to walk down the road and round to where I had parked the car. In the midst of my frightening experience, I had totally forgotten about my own special make up and dress mode. That is until a couple drove past and lit me up in their headlights.

The car turned around about half a mile down the road and they came back for a second look, slowing down as they passed. The guy was laughing but the woman had a concerned look on her face. They almost came to a stop about a hundred yards ahead and seemed to be waiting for me to catch them up. Out of devilment, I broke into a gallop and ran towards them screaming and waving my arms! I heard the girl scream as the guy put his foot down and did nought to sixty in about five seconds....... not bad for a Ford Escort!'

Well, as you can imagine, the topic of conversation in the pub that Sunday lunchtime hardly moved away from the subject of ghostly events. It was obvious that Ian had undergone a very emotional experience and we all agreed that there were things out there that we still didn't understand and that we should show a lot more respect in future.

George the bar manager poured Ian a large brandy on the house and casually enquired if anyone else had actually come into physical contact with a ghost. Local farmhand Mickey Wallace was first to put his hand up and shouted, 'yes! I shagged one once'.

With half the pub looking at Mickey, George said, 'you actually made love to a ghost?' Mickey apologetically put his hand down and explained, 'sorry, I thought you said a goat!'

Later, as I stood out in the gents, trying to drown whatever it was that was flying around my urinal, Ian came out and stood next to me. I casually said to him, 'God moves in mysterious ways mate, I can only imagine what you must have felt like when you saw that apparition of the 'Grey Lady'.' He looked at me and smiled and said, 'what!....... you as well?'

.

Chapter five: Luton airport

That was the end of my ghost hunting adventures and I have some great memories of the characters involved. That really sums up my attitude to life in those days. You are only young once and that's the time to sow a few wild oats. There's no way of telling where life is going to lead us so why not explore a few avenues along the way. I sometimes look back on the next couple of incidents and wonder if I actually went through a period of insanity in my late teens. If my father was alive today, he would certainly endorse those suspicions.

I had missed 'Flower Power and Free Love' and listened with envy to the fantastic music of The Move and Jimmy Hendrix along with people's recollections of music festivals, parties and wild happenings. In a way, I suppose I must have felt cheated and needed to display some kind of rebel image to show that my generation also had something to say.

Not being of the 'large muscular' variety, I often found myself compensating for lack of size by being 'more daring' or 'reckless' than the others. Especially if there were any challenges thrown down at the end of an alcohol fuelled session down the pub..

The conversation could not have been more innocent, but the end result will stagger you. If someone told me this story I would be suspicious to say the least, but this really happened.

'Unemployment is on the increase again' said Ian as we entered the final hour's drinking that night. That's the period you can't normally remember the next day.

To this day I have no idea why I took up the gauntlet on behalf of the hard working man, but I found myself saying, 'there's plenty of work out there!.....you just need to get off your backside and go looking for it. They shouldn't give out all this unemployment money the way they do, there's no incentive for people to work!'

Well that was it! 'It's alright for you, sitting in your office training to be an architect,' said Ian and a couple of other like minded people.

'Hold on! I went to the same school as you lot and chose a career which was within the scope of my ability. If I hadn't been good at maths and technical drawing I would have been just as happy training to be a bricklayer or a carpenter.'

A bloke sitting near us said, 'yeah, but those opportunities don't exist in every area, there just aint enough jobs to go round in some places.'

Before I could stop myself I replied, 'rubbish, I could go anywhere and get a job and then work my way up the ladder.....anywhere at all!'

There was some laughter and then a voice called out, 'okay, let's see you go to Luton and get a job.'

The bastard had chosen Luton because he knew that a massive car manufacturing factory had recently shut down and put several thousand people on the dole.'

I had talked myself into a noose. 'Okay, what's the bet ?'

'No money......just bet you can't do it. If you think that it's that easy, let's see you go and do it,' they goaded me.

The next day I gave my notice in at Bostocks and told mum and dad that I was leaving home. My father never swore much but he made an exception for me that day. I'd be a liar if I didn't admit to laying in bed wondering what on earth I had done. But I couldn't lose face and they had already arranged a farewell party for me down the pub. Cake and everything, so there was no backing out.

Eight days later, I found myself standing, suitcase in hand, on the platform of Luton station. My optimism had led to me purchasing a one way ticket. It was going to be a long walk home if my optimism turned into floptimism!

As I stood there in the pouring rain watching the train disappearing into the distance, I decided that I needed a drink. I found a pub and got chatting to one of the bar staff about job prospects. He confirmed that it would not be easy and suggested hanging around the local airport and keeping an eye on notice boards and shop windows of the various services available.

I didn't have much money to spare and in the absence of an income was wondering how much a 'cheap' room was going to cost me.

My new found friend behind the bar had already worked that one out as well. He told me to

45

go to the long term car park at the airport and try the back doors of hatchbacks and estate cars. He said that I was bound to find one open but to check the dates on the ticket to make sure that the owners would not be returning that night.

That is how I came to spend three nights sleeping in the back of a Vauxhall Viva estate car. The three days were spent trudging around the various terminals looking for a job. On the fourth day my luck changed! I got a job washing cars for Hertz car rental services.

The guy who was vacating the position had been renting a room in a house nearby, so I was able to take his place there as well. Brilliant a new job and somewhere to live, both on the same day.

I became friends with another guy who was lodging at the same house. His name was Phil Thorne and I went on to share many a night on the 'amber brew' with him. We would often sit and discuss our various dreams and aspirations and would always end up being rich and famous.

After being at Hertz a few weeks and getting to know the way of things, I became aware that there were areas of inefficiency within the existing system. Most could be improved, if handled by someone with a mathematical brain and two eyes. I would emphasize that the mathematical ability required was probably the equivalent of an eleven plus student!

Under the existing system, if a rented car broke down or would not start for any reason, the client was having to wait for a private breakdown company to take them and the car to the nearest garage to be repaired. On many occasions, it was noted that starting difficulties had been the result of carburettor flooding. A common problem with petrol engines in those days.

Consequently, Hertz would often end up with a dissatisfied customer, and having to pay out compensation for a spoilt holiday, overnight hotel costs, plus repair and call out charges equivalent to around £200.00 by today's prices.

It became obvious to me that the only person who could possibly sort this problem out, was the little guy washing cars round the back of the car park.

I asked for a meeting with the management and put my proposal forward.

My suggestion was that as soon as the breakdown or malfunction was reported, someone from the nearest depot, would take a replacement vehicle to the client. This would minimise the interruption to their holiday and save a small fortune on having to pay a garage minimum call out fee of £50.00, merely for them to start the engine first time because it had been flooded due to over exuberance on the accelerator.

I then took my proposal one stage further by suggesting that the person taking the replacement vehicle, should carry a toolbox and be trained in basic roadside diagnosis and repairs. It had long been realised that only a small percentage of calls received actually resulted in full scale garage repairs being required. It subsequently became clear that many of the garages called out had been abusing the system by submitting inflated, false accounts of minor problems and charging extortionate rates.

My suggestion was put to the Hertz head office, which was situated at Heathrow airport. They sent for me and I explained exactly how the scheme would work. They loved the idea and paid for me to go on a 'trouble shooting/get it started' course.

On completion of my training, I was given a state of the art set of tools and various meters needed to carry out on the spot diagnosis and repair work. I was promoted to Recovery Manager at Luton airport and given a new car for my own personal use.

I will always remember my first 'recovery' assignment. A car had refused to start in St Albans and the customers wanted it sorted double quick. I was there in under an half an hour and they drove off in the replacement car that I had given them. As they drove away, satisfied that their inconvenience had been minimised, I got into their first car and turned the key. The car started immediately and I drove it back to Luton, arriving in time for the morning tea break. There was nothing wrong with the car, the people had simply flooded the carburettor. As previously mentioned this was a common problem with many of the modern petrol engines. Too much choke and enthusiasm on the accelerator meant waiting for it to dry out, which would often take several minutes.

Another pain in the proverbial was immobiliser switches. These were becoming popular and people were saving fortunes on insurance premiums if their car had an immobiliser fitted. The problem was that not every client was aware that they were driving a car with a built in automatic immobiliser It activated when the car was vacated and locked. Upon re-entry it needed to be de-activated before starting. This would normally be achieved by touching a switch or button under the dashboard.

With my knowledge of the last two items alone, I was able to solve almost 50% of all breakdown calls over the phone. I continued to learn as much as possible about trouble shooting minor problems and soon became aware that various models and makes had their own particular problem area. This made it a lot easier for me to quickly remedy the problem and I set about saving Hertz a lot of money.

I had made my mark with Hertz and would undoubtedly have climbed the ladder to top management over the years. Sadly, our relationship came to an abrupt end in the most unfortunate of circumstances.

As mentioned earlier, I had been given a very expensive tool kit....it was my pride and joy.

I had repaired an immobiliser switch on a vehicle and driven it back to our depot. I put the all clear label on it to indicate to sales that the vehicle was ready for rental. I had worked quite late in order to finish the job that evening and went home, forgetting that I had left my toolbox in the boot of the repaired vehicle.

As I clocked off that evening, one of the managers asked me if I could accompany him to Heathrow first thing in the morning and drive a vehicle back to Luton. He said that he would pick me up at my lodgings. The next day, I got back to Luton at around 11am and parked the car. Now my nightmare began. Whilst having a cup of tea, a guy from sales told me that the car I had repaired the night before had gone out on rental! My tool box was still in the boot!

We managed to contact the client at 4pm. He was up in Sheffield. He had booked the car for a fortnight and I needed my tools urgently. With the manager's approval I jumped into my car and drove back to my lodgings. Had a quick wash and bite to eat and prepared to drive up to Yorkshire.

On the way out I bumped into my fellow lodger Phil Thorne and told him where I was off to. He offered to come along to keep me company, so off we went.

We found the address in Sheffield and picked up the box of tools. We had a meal and a cup of tea and set off back to Luton.

The weather conditions were deteriorating fast. It was becoming extremely foggy on the M1 and black ice was developing as the surface begun to freeze. We were making good time and had reached Northampton when suddenly, up ahead I saw a couple of cars sliding and swerved to avoid them. Before I knew it I was on the black ice and going sideways. I attempted to straighten up but was now going backwards. As I hit the kerb of the hard shoulder, the car flipped over and rolled down the embankment into a field. The car was on its roof and we were battered and bruised....but still alive. The next few minutes will stay engraved into my mind until I die. As Phil and I painfully struggled to get out of the car, we could hear the terrible sounds above us as cars and lorries crashed into each other. Then, the sky lit up as a vehicle burst into flames. It was a multiple pile up.

The emergency services arrived and got us out of our vehicle. An ambulance took us to hospital, where we remained for 48 hours.. We were both bruised and badly shaken up but incredibly there were no limbs broken. The car however, was a write off.

We later learned that the pile up had stretched back for almost a mile. Sadly, there had been fatalities and it was one of the worst pile ups recorded at that time. We saw the pictures in the newspapers and realised how lucky we had been. When you lose control of a vehicle on ice, it is a very frightening experience and you really are in the lap of the gods.

Hertz were very good and supportive......until they got a letter from the insurance company. They refused to pay out because I was under twenty one. I was in fact just nineteen years old!

Hertz had seen my driving license and not spotted my age. I was not aware of the criteria for driving their vehicles. Remember, I had only come to wash cars! There had been no age restrictions in that department. It was just an unfortunate oversight on everyone's part. There was no way that I could afford to pay for the car. They had no choice but to sack me.

I had proved my point and won my bet with the lads in the pub, but I was unemployed again. Phil hated his job as a cook's assistant in a hotel. They said that he had been working as a freelance and refused to pay him for being off sick, so we decide to go home to Margate and Whitstable.

On the way home I saw an advert in the daily paper. 'This is the one for us Phil,' I shouted. 'They need gofers in the Munich Olympic Games.'

'Is that Munich in Germany?' asked Phil.

I looked at him and smiled, 'yes! but don't worry about it.....I've got a cunning plan.'

The look on my mum's and dad's face when I turned up on the doorstep, was a picture.

Dad had always tried to be supportive throughout my life, but he had been at a loss trying to understand why I'd packed in a perfectly good job, with a future, to go gallivanting around Luton.

As we sat and drank tea, there was a sense of relief in the air. Mum was cooking me a fry up. I had come home safe and sound. Now, having got all the silliness out of my system, it was time to decide what profession I was contemplating for the future. Things could get back to normal.

Let the history books show that the year I had been away, was merely a sabbatical and that I had returned to the fold physically and mentally prepared for the serious stuff. It was natural that my parents should think that way

As I dipped my bread into the yolk of a fried egg, mum was fussing round me as if she were the mother hen that had laid it.

'What do you have in mind now, son? Do you think that Bostocks might take you back? Where do you see the future, Barry?' Dad was seriously interested and mum was hanging on my every word. So try to picture the look on both their faces as I shoved half a pork sausage in my mouth and uttered the word, 'Munich'.

'Who are they?' asked mum in all innocence, 'have you got an interview with them?'

Dad on the other hand was slightly agitated. 'Do you mean Munich in Germany?'

Trying to be funny I replied, 'is there any other?'

Dad closed his eyes and sat back in his chair. I hadn't even told them why I wanted to go to Munich, they didn't know what was waiting for me out there. Come to that, neither did I.

At this point in the conversation it wouldn't have mattered if the chairmanship of Volkswagen was waiting for me out there. All that mattered at this point was the fact that the last time my father was out in Munich there had been a million Germans trying to kill him.

In his efforts to stay calm, my father took a deep breath and asked, What's the attraction in Munich?'

A spoon full of baked beans gave me the strength I needed to say, 'The Olympic Games.'

Mum's eyes opened wide and my father sat forward in his chair. He was now about twelve inches from my face.

'But you're not in the Olympic bloody games, what are you going to do in Munich?' I detected a touch of agitation in his voice.

'They need gofers out there.' I muttered nervously.

'But you don't play golf!' said mum with a worried look on her face.

'Gofers mum, people.......people who go for things'.

'What sort of things? I've never heard of people like that before. You do worry me sometimes, Barry.'

Dad stood up and walked away from the table. Without even turning round he sarcastically said to mum, 'dogsbodies! people who fetch and carry things, wonderful, real job with a future if ever I heard of one, the Olympic Games last about two months.....then nothing for four years...... what then?'

I must confess that I hadn't really thought that far ahead. I was aware of the Open Golf Championship being up at Gleneagles that year but wasn't sure of the date......or if they would need gofers? The prospect of having 'Golfing Gofer' on my CV flashed through my mind. But I decided not to share that one with my dad....well, not at this moment in time anyway.   Come to think of it, who goes and picks up all those balls from the practice range?

One week later, I kissed my tearful mum and shook dads reluctant hand again before walking up the road with a rucksack on my back and a bacon sandwich in my pocket.

I met Phil at Margate Station and we made our way to Dover. We caught a ferry to Zeebrugge and proceeded to hitchhike across Belgium and Holland staying at all kinds of overnight haunts. including a school caretakers house, a nightclub, and two hay lofts. After eight days we crossed the border into Germany and made it as far as Dusseldorf.

We were hitch hiking out way to Munich and were just approaching Dusseldorf when a police car pulled up. The two officers looked at our piece of cardboard with the word Munich scribbled in pencil. They laughed and jabbered away and we heard the word Munich mentioned. 'What they saying Baz?' said Phil, who believed I could speak German because I knew the words Doberman Pincer. They looked at us and said 'Munich Ya?' Ya....Ya....I said, nodding enthusiastically. They opened the door to the police car and indicated for us to climb in and muttered something else that contained the word Munich, they were still smiling. As we climbed aboard I said the other words that I knew in German, danken schon!

As we pulled away I could see that Phil was well impressed with my word power, 'what's happening Baz?' he asked as I nodded and smiled at the police officer sitting in the passenger seat, who was smiling and muttering Munich over and over again. I could no longer hide my elation. I looked at Phil and said. 'They're only gonna drive us to fucking Munich Phil, that's all! Now at this point in the story I would draw your attention to a map of Germany. You will notice two things. One is that Dusseldorf is barely just inside the Dutch/German border. Now if you look across you will see Munich...that's it! just before you reach Austria.........about five hundred miles away.

We were in the police car for approx five minutes when it pulled into a car park and we were asked to step out again. Phil looked at me, 'I don't believe it, we were that close and we never knew!'

He grabbed the police officers hand and shook it rigorously....Dunky John he said out loud. The officer smiled and indicated for us to walk through a doorway leading into a large hall. 'Ah, not a cup of tea as well,' said Phil, as we walked through into the main office of the police station. After producing our passports and being questioned for an hour we were introduced to an interpreter. She was a lovely girl who explained that there was nothing to worry about. As the two officers prepared to go back on duty, they turned and jabbered something to her. They then smiled at us and said auf Wiedersehen as they walked away. Dunky John...Dunky John, shouted Phil. The nice young lady was flicking through the pages of her translation book and laid it in front of me.

'Okay! please tell me how you pronounce this word, is it docilee?' I looked at the word, 'no, you pronounce that docile....docile!' 'Thank you, and what about this one, how do you say this one, is it prartis'. I followed her finger. 'No! that one is pratts' I volunteered. 'Okay, thank you. So, they are saying, tell this pair of docile pratts to go back where they came from and not to come to Germany again without work permits or they will be arrested.'

Our brief period as guest of the German Bunderspolizei (border police) Public Relations dept, dampened our enthusiasm somewhat. Ten days later, feeling very leg weary, I walked into the kitchen of our house and cuddled my mum.

That evening, as we sat down to have dinner together. Dad could see that I was a bit crestfallen so he didn't need to lecture or say 'I told you so'. He got the beers out and we laughed at some of the events that had occurred on my fruitless journey.

'Where are you off to next?' asked dad with a smile on his face. 'The Amazon basin looks interesting!'

'Well, I thought I might stick around for a bit, try my luck in England dad, Margate preferably!'

'Why, what's made you decide that?' said mum.

'Well, apart from wearing my legs out, I can't afford the shoe repair bills anymore,' I laughed.

I laid in the next morning, it had been the first time I'd slept in a proper bed for a week.

Chapter six: Barry the bookie

The next day as we sat down to breakfast, dad laid the local paper in front of me. 'There's something that might interest you son. I think you'd be good at that,' he said as he walked away.

'But I don't know anything about delivering babies dad.....I'd never make a good midwife!' I shouted as he started to walk up the stairs.

'Look at the one underneath.........trainee bookmaker opportunity!', he replied.

I was just wiping the last piece of bread round my plate. 'I don't know anything about making books either.'

I took a closer look at the paper. It was an advert for a trainee manager with Mecca bookmakers. The vacancy was in their local shop at Margate harbour.

I got an interview and quickly made it clear that all I knew about horses was that one end ate hay and the other end was best avoided .....for a variety of reasons.

The manager was a very nice gentleman and explained that I need have no concerns about only having equestrian experience on a rocking horse. Can you add up and take away?, he asked.

'Yes I can,' I replied.

'Have you ever done any thieving?', he asked with a smile.

'Not yet, but I'm willing to give it a go if it will help,' I laughed!

His face developed a more serious look.

'I was only joking,' I quickly added. 'I think that all thieves are scum and they should have their hands chopped off.........or be castrated even!'

He gave me a surprised look over the top of his glasses and I remember praying that he wasn't a thief!

I sensed that things were getting too serious so I quickly enquired, 'what about time off?'

He nodded in a meaningful way, 'you can have as much time off as you like, as long as it's between 6pm and 9 am.'

'There's no point in my going anywhere then,' I laughed, 'by the time I get there it will be shut and nearly time to come home.'

'You've got a point there, but think of the money you will be saving,' he scoffed.

I tucked my shirt in and pulled myself up to my full height. 'I've already saved the money....I want to spend it on a holiday.'

'Christmas, Summer and Easter; it adds up to six weeks a year on full pay once you have finished training.'

I could see that he was being serious again so I thanked him and shook his hand.

I was twenty years old. It was time to start taking life more seriously....think of the future. I thanked him and made my way to the nearest pub. I was half way through my second pint when it dawned on me. Of course, this is it. This is where I am meant to be. God moves in mysterious ways. It all makes sense now! The pub was only two doors away from the betting shop!

Less than a week later, I commenced working at Mecca's betting shop in Kings Street Margate harbour. It was to be the beginning of an incredible journey. Thanks to the love and patience of my parents, I was right where I was always meant to be.....doing what I was always meant to do. I was growing taller by the minute!

I took to bookmaking like a fish to water. Boring, it was not. I loved the characters, the atmosphere and the repartee. I had always enjoyed maths and settling bets was an easy learning curve. I was taught all sorts of formulas and short cuts and before long, you could give me the prices of four winners in a Yankee and before you could say, 'How Much?' I would put a piece of paper in front of you with the total winnings on! Settlers today? They don't know they're born! Press a button....there it is. But God help them if the computer goes down!

It took me six months to become a manager and run my own shop.

It took me six weeks to realize that gambling is a mug's game.......if you don't play it right!

Over the years, I have seen fortunes gambled recklessly by people chasing lost money. Instead of cutting and running whilst they're ahead, they think that they can beat the system. The saddest punters of all are the stubborn ones who stand and challenge the omens.

We all have a bad day once in a while and we normally know when it's arrived. It usually becomes quite evident after our first three bets go down the pan that we should have stayed at home and watched the telly. Losing your beer and fags money for the week is one thing, but I've seen guys lose the rent and mortgage money.

Many high rollers often get off to a good start and you can't blame them for thinking that maybe this is going to be 'their day?' If I hadn't been there to make money for my company, I could quite easily have put a notice above the counter in big letters. 'BEWARE! Suck You In Blow You Out!'

I've watched punters go two grand up in the first fifteen minutes and then be two grand down ten minutes later. It's only a question of time. The sensibility of quitting while you're ahead is rapidly overshadowed by the favourite in the 3.30 looking a certainty! But then again, if all punters behaved 'sensibly' there wouldn't be loads of wealthy bookmakers. I have laughed many times at guys who pick up a few quid and wave in my face. 'Aha! I'm playing with your money now,' they sneer.

I smile and say 'good luck to you.' But deep inside I'm saying, 'don't get too excited mate....it's only a loan! I'll be getting it back with interest.'

Believe it or not, a good win is good for business, especially in a busy shop. Advertising on telly cost millions every year. Fair enough, that's a tax man situation I admit, spend it or give it to them. But it can never compete with Joe Public picking up £800.00 for a 50p e/w Yankee. An £11 bet for the cost of five and a half National Lottery tickets. I take that winning Yankee ticket and make three photocopies. I put one in the window, one above the counter and one above the drinks machine. Winnings on multibets often run into thousands of pounds and are well within reach of all punters. An each way Yankee is a 22 possible money winning combination bet. Do that each Saturday for a year and you would have to be extremely unlucky not to have a few nice pickups during that time.

The odds on winning over £100 on a Lottery ticket are astronomical by comparison. I once had four numbers plus the bonus number in a line. The bonus number counted for sweet sod all and I picked up £86.00, my biggest win on the lottery after almost seventeen years at a fiver a week. What a joke! For 50p more, I could have picked out four horses and done a 50p win or a 25p e/w Yankee every week. For seventeen years??......the mind boggles.

The friendliest family bet in my opinion is a ten pence e/w Heinz. Pick out six horses. That represents 57 win and 57 place combinations. If none of them win but four of them finish in the first three at 20/1, that's 11 place wins at quarter odds, equals £230.40.pay out. How many opportunities in life do you know whereby you can pick up £230.40 for £11.40 without picking a winner? Plus you get a better run for your money (literally) than you do with the lottery which is over and done within seconds. I once saw a £14,000-00 payout on a ten pence e/w Canadian.

All five horses won, with two of them being 33/1 and one at 25/1. The other two were hot favourites. Even if the two favourites had lost, the payout was still over three thousand pounds. Also, if the three outsiders had only finished in the first three and the favourites lost, there was still almost £80.00 to pick up. For the record, a ten pence e/w Canadian cost £5.20. That doesn't even buy you three lottery tickets today! I know which one is the best **bet** in my opinion.

Whilst we're on the subject, I have emphasised the word bet because I have always considered that there is a substantial difference between a bet and a gamble. Don't get me wrong, I'm fully aware that if you invest money in something with the possibility of losing it, then it is a gamble.

However, I imagine that most people would object to being labelled 'habitual gamblers' just because they buy three lottery tickets each week. It's the same principle though!

As I have already stated earlier, I think that a nice little bet, say once a week, is a ten pence e/w Canadian. £5.20p. Same principle involved i.e. you walk in, pay your money, pick up your ticket and walk out. Going shopping or to the football in the afternoon, you come home and look up the results or, you can watch your horses run on TV. Win or lose, that's it until next week! 26 possible winning combinations for less than the price of two pints of lager. Do that 52 weeks a year and it will knock the National Lottery into a cocked hat!

Gambling, is when you stand in a shop chasing losings, doubling your bet because you are convinced that your luck is about to change. Going home stressed out and having to face the wife or wondering how you are going to get to and from work next week? Untold pressure from something that is meant to be a bit of fun.

Successful professional gamblers rarely step inside a betting shop. They certainly don't stand there all day trying to pick the winner of every race.

They watch races and study times, ground conditions, stable form, right down to when a horse had its last crap. After all that, if they can get 2/1 or 3/1 on a horse that, by their reckoning should be even money favourite on the day, they put five or ten grand on the nose. Win or lose they walk away. Some top professionals only have a dozen or so bets a year!

Most betting shops have gambling machines these days. Anything from Roulette to Pontoon.

You can win a lot of money. But you can lose a lot of money! I have watched people lose their whole week's wages in one session. The machine keeps the punter happy with a few £20, £50, £75 or £100 wins along the way but greed or stupidity makes them put it all back in again as they chase that elusive 'Big One'.

These machines don't just make the roulette ball land on zero when it suits them. That's the easy part. If that machine could attend university, it would achieve a double first with honours in psychology and economics. The reason being that the sequence programme installed is built around years of research having been fed into a computer with the instruction, 'Go Get'em!' With every press of the button, it knows exactly what is going through the mind of the punter and is designed to play on basic human reaction. Greed, regret, anger, jubilation and the players own predictable strange form of logic......I'll explain.

Guy puts forty pounds in the machine and wins twenty five pounds on the fortieth go. As far as he is concerned, the machine still has fifteen pounds of his money......he wants it back. He puts in another thirty pounds and wins another twenty five. That's a far better ratio. But then, the weirdest thing happens! Because the punter is looking for a comfort zone, he suddenly reasons that because he has won fifty pounds in the last thirty goes, he has recovered the fifteen pounds deficit and has gone five pounds up!........Really? By my calculations he's put in seventy pounds and won fifty! That means he is now twenty pounds down. That sounds weird but it really happens

If you stand there for ten hours with a dustbin full of money, no matter how much you are up at various times throughout that period.....more often than not, greed and stupidity will cause you to lose the lot! Okay, you both start the day with a shed load of money but you will never ever be as good at taking it from the machine as it is at taking it from you. To use a racing term......'That is a stone bonking certainty mate.' Believe me when I tell you this. You don't play the machine......the machine plays you!

Kicking the machine, screaming abuse at the shop staff or breaking the toilet door off doesn't change that. On the contrary! It confirms our earlier suspicions that you are a brainless moron. You were one hundred quid up at one time, why didn't you take it and run? Take my advice, put ten pounds or so into the machine. Win or lose, walk away. Like so many other aspects of life, it's all about being in the right place at the right time.

Talking of morons! Did you know that gambling machines in betting shops and clubs are the most frequently used tools by drug dealers to launder money? It's no big secret. The police know that it is happening. Problem is, knowing it and proving it are two different things.

Here's another comforting fact to consider. Over half the paper money in circulation has traces of drugs on it. Consequently, it can no longer be submitted in a court of law as evidence of handling by a suspected drug dealer.

I grew up very quickly when I started working for Mecca and my sense of responsibility developed literally overnight. My father was pleased that I had settled down into a job that had a good future. His older brother, Nobby Coombs, was a bookie. My father also took comfort from the fact that it was he who had drawn my attention to the advert in the first place. By the age of twenty one, against all the odds, I had become a man!

Some years earlier I was having a drink with brother David and casually asked him, 'when will I know that I have become a man?' He pondered for a few seconds and replied. 'I think it's when you can walk into a pub anywhere in England.....look along the names on the pumps.......and know exactly which ones you like!' I was sixteen at the time and remember using that information as a rule of thumb for the next two years. It got to the stage whereby you could name any pub in Kent and I could tell you what draught beer they sold. I was a walking pub guide. You could go a long way with knowledge like that! Well, certainly all over Kent! But I didn't become a complete man until I joined Mecca......read on.

Bookmakers don't like to see anyone lose their weeks wages gambling. That is bad for the industry and it builds resentment. Yes, of course we like it when people lose a few quid and I'd be a liar if I didn't admit that the best feeling of all is when someone wins a few hundred quid during the afternoon and then comes and gives it back to us in the evening. At least they got to know what it felt like to have a lucky streak! Because that's what it was!

Like smoking and drinking, gambling can be addictive. It often makes people do silly things. In most cases, if you burn your fingers, you take time off for the wounds to heal. As the memories fade you look at the paper one day and say, there's a couple of horses I fancy at Newbury today, think I'll pop into Mecca whilst we're out shopping and do a little five pounds e/w double! Fine! Go home, put your feet up and say a little prayer that they both win at twenty to one. No harm done.

Then, there's the addict! I call them crusaders! They look upon gambling as an all out war. Us against them. They are the ones who can't help themselves. You could tell them that you've had a telephone call from the trainer saying that the even money favourite in the two thirty was going to romp home and they would still put a tenner on the 5/1 shot. They push their way past you as you open on Saturday morning, muttering something stupid like, 'It owes me a hundred and fifty quid from last week!' 'IT' being the roulette machine.......that's right, the one in the corner sobbing its heart out. So full of remorse that it can't wait for the opportunity to send you home in your pants and vest!

Take my advice. Work out how much you can afford to lose....say ten pounds! Put it in the machine....win or lose, walk away. As I said earlier, like most things in life 90% of good fortune is about being in the right place at the right time.

By the way, you might think it strange for a person trained in upper management in the betting industry to be pointing out some of this information. It might also interest you to know that I have experienced every emotion felt by the punters reading this book.

Over the years I have been guilty of taking some incredible chances. Yes, there have been a few champagne occasions. A day at the races with a few friends is great fun. Have a few bets, a drink and a meal and relish the memories of picking a few winners. But sometimes those winners can be hard to find. When that seemingly underpriced 8/1 shot tempts your confident £10 e/w wager, only to stroll home ten minutes later in last position, the expletives voiced on such occasions would suggest a mistake on your part. I have also made a few mistakes, one of which was absolutely disastrous. Believe me lads and ladies, I know exactly how it feels to look in a mirror and say to the idiot staring back, 'Oh my God! What have you done?'

Chapter seven: Business with pleasure

Upon reaching manager status in the early part of 1973, I was used as a relief manager by Mecca. Covering for illness and holidays etc, it was the best possible preparation I could have had for the years and events that would follow.

Moving from shop to shop, I learned the skills required to become a top manager. How to earn recognition and respect by being good at what I was doing. Handling initial resentment and coping with comments such as 'you're not our manager.' Knowing when to laugh and encourage and when to wield the big stick. I can think back to a couple of shops where the resentment and disrespect towards me was so bad, I could have sacked them all. But I gradually learned that the quickest way forward was to show them that I could do everything being asked of them, but do it twice as fast and twice as good. One shop in particular had a terrible atmosphere behind the counter and the turnover was rock bottom when I took over as the new relief manager. This was to become a massive learning curve for me.

The regular manager was in hospital, due to a road accident. Nothing life threatening but a few weeks' convalescence was on the cards. I was sent to take over for as long as it would take for him to get back on his feet again.

On my first day, I ran into hostility from the female assistant manager who resented my being there. She more or less told the other staff that as far as they were concerned she was boss. I later discovered that this was also the case when the permanent manager was there. She was a loud mouthed bully and was the reason why the shop was struggling.

By the end of my first week, I had watched her being rude to customers, making threatening gestures to her fellow staff members and had endured no end of verbal abuse to myself. The final straw occurred on Friday afternoon when her husband came into the shop at 3.30pm. He stunk of beer and B.O. and was abusive to her. There followed a slanging match between them which almost emptied the shop.

I ordered him off the premises and was threatened with a punch on the nose from him and told to mind my own business by her. He eventually left when I picked up the phone to call the police. Apparently, he was well known to them and was on probation at the time.

That evening I spoke to my Area Manager who I admired tremendously. He had been a great influence during my training and had always told me to contact him immediately if I had any problems. I had been with the company over three years and this was the first time I had felt a bit out of my depth. I explained that I could no longer work with this women who I considered was not right for the job. Also, I wanted to bar her husband from the shop without getting myself killed. I had read my contract and there was nothing about rolling around in the street with a drunken nutter.

I also said that, in my opinion, the shop had far greater potential than it was showing at present and gave a few reasons as to why this was the case.

I think that this was my first real experience of the relief felt as a result of that old adage 'a trouble shared'.

I managed to get through the following day (Saturday) even though I did feel as though I was walking on eggshells for a time. There were still a few disrespectful comments flying about but she did mention that she had warned her husband to stay away. I won't tell you what she said to him in case any children pick up this book, but it would certainly have curtailed any future thoughts he might have had about re-production!

At 10 o'clock on Monday morning, my Area Manager walked into the shop accompanied by a young girl who was wearing the new Mecca blouse. She looked about sixteen and I suddenly felt very old.

He immediately suspended the assistant manager on full pay pending enquiries of misconduct and violent behaviour. Her face turned to a sneer but before she could utter a word he spoke again. 'Before you say anything, there is an alternative. You can be sacked on the spot and be escorted off the premises. I strongly recommend that you say nothing at this stage. Furthermore, neither you or any member of your family are to enter these premises until further notice and any attempt to do so will result in the police being called. Please pick up your personal possessions and leave the shop now. We will be in touch with you shortly.'

The mentality of the women was clear to see. Obviously, quite happy to have no personal income during the foreseeable future, she burned her bridges as she left by shouting, 'You can poke your fucking shop you pair of arseholes.'

As she stormed off down the road, the Area Manager and I looked at each other and burst out laughing. 'Well that's made all our jobs a lot easier,' he laughed.

The atmosphere in the shop changed overnight and you could sense the relief felt by all. The new assistant proved to be an absolute diamond and it was a pleasure to work with. She was as bright as a button and eager to learn. It was my first experience of training a new recruit and I couldn't have asked for a better pupil. I later heard through the pipeline that she went on to become one of the youngest betting shop managers on the circuit.

I managed the shop for almost six months, during which time bully girl and her smelly husband never showed their faces. She was obviously sacked and received no references.

During my time there, I had more than doubled the weekly turnover and improved the shop atmosphere tenfold. My final month in charge was with the original manager back on part time duty as assistant manager. He was a nice enough man and relieved that bully girl had gone, but he should never have allowed the situation to develop to such a serious level. It was obvious to me that he would never make top manager material.

As far as I am concerned, the training and support I received from Mecca was second to none. I simply passed on to my staff the words of wisdom that had been imparted to me from day one. Always remember, it's the public who pay your wages!

Rule One. Make your regular customers feel part of a family. They are your bread and butter bets and well worth a smile when paying them out a nice win now and then. A cup of coffee when things are a bit quiet goes a long way with most people. A two hundred pound pick up is a big day for most 'family' punters and will become good publicity for you when the winner tells the other thirty people working at their factory.

It was not long after that incident, that I was rewarded with my first permanent shop. None other than Kings Street, Margate. The shop I had been trained at just over three years earlier.

It couldn't have been better for me. Managing a shop ten minutes from where I lived. Mum and Dad had sold the guest house and bought a nice three bed mock Tudor semi. Enjoying a south facing garden, laid to lawn plus large vegetable garden with detached greenhouse. My father was a keen gardener and spent as much time as possible tending the large plot.

Obviously, having lived in Cliftonville since the age of nine, I knew quite a few of the regulars who used the betting shop. This resulted in my enjoying a hectic social life (No Night Racing in those days). In August 1976 I met my first wife, Yvette. Looking back I think it was a combination of love and lust at first sight. She was a 'looker' and would turn a few heads when we were out. I made David laugh on the phone one time when he asked me how a charity evening that I had organised at Dumpton Park dog Stadium had gone. I said that it had been a great night and that Yvette had won a trophy. He was quite surprised and asked in all innocence what the trophy had been awarded for. I told him it was the one awarded to the fastest bitch on the track. David laughed his head off and I got a slap from Yvette.

It was a whirlwind romance and we booked the wedding for the 11th December that year. At last my life was starting to level off and I was feeling settled for the first time. We bought a bungalow in a place called Dane Valley and spent time doing it up prior to the forthcoming marriage. Life was becoming very conventional.

Sadly, tragedy struck on the 12th November when my father died suddenly at home. He had not been ill and there was no reason to suspect that this would happen, but he had a massive coronary arrest. Yvette was there that evening and we had sat down and enjoyed dinner as a family. We discussed the bungalow and the last minute arrangements for the forthcoming wedding. Minutes later, he collapsed and died as my mother cradled him in her arms. He was 66 years old. I would be proud to be half the man he was.

Two weeks before my wedding, we buried my father. I don't remember hearing the church bells on either occasion. I felt completely numb and unable to accept that the finest man I'd ever known was gone. I had so much wanted to make him proud of me, but my achievement years were yet to come. My father has continued to be my inspiration to this day and I firmly believe that he has watched and smiled with approval at some of my efforts.

In these ever changing times, we often find ourselves reassessing our values and attitudes towards life, but there are some aspects that never change. My love for my fellow man and the criteria laid down by my parents, coupled with my belief in the Christian faith, are as strong

Someone once said that the path of true love never runs smooth. Many people describe their marriage as being, 'a bit rocky at times!' I hold my hands up and declare that my marriage to Yvette never ran smooth and as for 'a bit rocky', it made Mount Everest look like a billiard table! We shouldn't have got married!

Neither of us were ready for settling down and we both came to realise that we had made a serious mistake. I was a terrible husband and she was a terrible wife. However, there must have been a few amicable occasions (probably alcohol fuelled) because my son, Ben, was born in 1977 and my daughter, Chantelle, in 1979. Thanks to them I now have five beautiful grandchildren who all love me to pieces.

I looked upon marriage and its commitments as an occupational hazard. My happiest times were spent in my shop and down the pub. Reason being, I loved my work and I loved beer. How's that for honesty!

Okay! If we were really honest about it, yes I suppose we did love each other, plus we both scrubbed up well and had a good circle of friends.

But most of the time we would just be getting under each other's feet.

There had been some great parties over the years, but once we'd arrived, we went our own ways and didn't see each other until it was time to go home. I would get stuck into the amber nectar and a game of cards with the lads. And she...! Well, God knows what she was getting up to, but I never saw her until it was time to go home!

This would be a typical 'morning after', conversation that I recall quite well.

Time: 10am Sunday

Barry in kitchen making toast and coffee. In walks Yvette in dressing gown and slippers.

YVETTE: You still here?

BARRY: You never met anyone then?

YVETTE: No! still looking.....how much did you lose?

BARRY: I won fifteen quid!

YVETTE: Bloody hell, make a note of the date.

BARRY: I heard you was snogging one of Tony's sons, how old is he then?

YVETTE: How the hell should I know....I don't ask to see their birth certificates......twelve I think!'

BARRY: Don't talk daft, he's been working down the brewery for three years.

YVETTE: Well, what did you ask for? You could have made me a cup of coffee.

BARRY: Yeah! could have.

Picks up his coffee and toast and walks off into the lounge to catch up on 'Match of the Day.'

Now does that sound normal to you? Hardly a marriage made in heaven is it? There's enough in there to keep a marriage guidance councillor going for six months....... and that was on our honeymoon! ....(no, not really).

That woman could nag for England, she was never satisfied unless she was complaining about something. I can only ever remember one occasion when she was entitled to have a go at me. One occasion when I was wrong......and I'm man enough to admit it.

I admit that I was a bit out of order......alright, I was well out of order! It was Easter, 1980. I remember it well because it had been raining for two days. Bloody weather man got it wrong again. cuh! Also, I lost the bungalow !!

Now before you start pointing the finger and shouting, ahhh! see..... gambling's a mugs game! Let me explain.....just give me a few minutes to think about it..........Right! You see, I met this guy who told me that he ran a syndicate and due to unforeseen circumstances one of the members had dropped out..

Basically, it all revolved around investing my house in the joint purchase of a one year old foal that had the right credentials to win the English Derby two years later. It was un gelded so the stud fees would be worth a fortune. Well, because he liked me, he was going to give me first refusal on the vacancy.

Now I won't bore you with the details at this point, but I later learned that the guy whose place I took, was forty eight years old when he had his first heart attack. By sheer coincidence, it was the day he learned that he didn't own a car or a luxury yacht anymore!

I tried to make Yvette realise how lucky we were to have only lost a two bedroomed bungalow. Plus, we wouldn't have to worry about mortgage repayments anymore.

As we packed all our possessions into cardboard boxes, she insisted that although she felt sorry that the man had lost his yacht, and car and was in hospital, she found it difficult to take comfort from it. In fact, she did not feel lucky at all. Aren't women strange sometimes?

God moves in mysterious ways and fate took a hand. There was an empty flat, overlooking the sea above the Mecca shop in Whitstable. I made a phone call and we moved into the flat a week later......phew!

When I say 'overlooking the sea' I must admit that this particular aspect of the property was not immediately evident. The shop itself was halfway down the High Street. However, I discovered that if you climbed on top of the wardrobe and looked through the gap between

Boots the chemist and Mothercare, you could just about see it!........when the tide was in.

It turned out to be a very brief stay in Whitstable. Fifteen months later, just as we had got the flat looking nice, I received a phone call from head office.

I was asked to take over a shop in Gillingham. It was another trouble shooting job. The shop in question had gradually been dropping in turnover for some time and Mecca wanted it to be given the kiss of life! So, I puckered up my lips and accepted the challenge. I saw it as another good career move.

It was going to be a bit of a journey from Whitstable each day, but I was now almost in a position to purchase another house. I have always believed in fate and there have been many events in my life which have convinced me that someone watches over us, but what happened next was really weird.

I had been with Mecca almost eight years at this point and had never been to Gillingham in my life. On the day I started work at the shop, a For Sale board went up on the house next door. Spooky or what?......mind you, with retrospect, I suppose it could have been something personal! But I have to admit, it really freaked me out at the time. is it any wonder that I drink? (Any excuse).

I put in an offer for number 2 Barnsole Rd Gillingham and moved in approximately three months later. Okay, it put the kybosh on my daily fuel allowance.

The shop was in a bad way business wise but it was situated in a heavily built up area. I immediately saw the potential. My area manager came to see me on the first day and over a cup of tea he said to me. 'Barry, I think this shop has a lot of potential!' There you go, I wasn't the only one was I? All it needed was a few fresh ideas and an injection of happiness.

On my first Saturday morning I got a surprise. As I opened up the shop, in walked my brother David. He was now running the family building business which had been started by my father in 1946. David was born and raised in the East End of London and was as street wise as.........something that.......lives in the street!! He took one look around the shop and said, 'do you know what Baz? I think this place has got a load of potential.'

I didn't want to hurt his feelings so I replied, 'really! Do you really think so?'

With his hands in his pockets he walked round the shop, nodding his head and muttering, 'yeah.....oh, yeah, I'll tell you what's needed to spark a bit of life into the old place Baz. Get a few women in here........ dress 'em up a bit.....put on some background music.

I smiled, 'Dave, it's a betting shop not a bloody knocking shop.'

He put his hand up. 'No! Hear me out bruv. I know where I can lay my hands on a job lot of meat pies and some crates of beer. Just stick a promotional sign in the window. Under new management. Managers special: Pie and a Pint and a Woman for the Night.......Fifteen quid...... You'll have'em queuing up mate.

He took a Steak and Kidney pie out of his jacket pocket and offered me a bite!....it was bloody horrible! 'It won't work with these pies' I sighed.

'The women will be disappointed.......maybe next year,' he laughed.

All that just to tell a joke!

The Gillingham shop was a major challenge. It was in a very 'tired' condition, and had fallen behind some of our main competitors who had 'modern' shops within striking distance. As a result, we had lost a large number of punters who were prepared to travel further afield to enjoy the latest facilities.

At my suggestion, the shop was given a facelift and an injection of 'sunshine & happiness from yours truly. By the end of year one, I had doubled the pre-Barry turnover.

I liked Gillingham because it represented a fresh start opportunity for me and Yvette. For a while we both worked hard at keeping the marriage going. Ben was growing up fast and Chantelle was now 'out of nappies'. Strange the things you remember isn't it. 'Out of nappies!'. That was a phrase I'd often heard my mother use when referring to people's children. Having established that it wasn't a follow on statement to, 'that reminds me, I must pop into Mothercare she's used up all her nappies,' I came to realise that it was a really good way of projecting a picture into someone's mind when they enquired, 'how's the baby getting on?'

'Yeah great!........he's out of nappies you know. Strange isn't it, but you never hear anyone answer, 'Yeah, great! He's into pants you know.' They take it for granted that you knew he was previously in nappies. Unless the poor sod was running around in his bare arse, with his willy hanging out!

Talking about willies! That's another thing I've noticed over the years. When Auntie Ivy pops in and picks up the baby from his playpen, she holds him up in the air and rambles on about, 'who's got big blues eyes then.....who's got two big dimples in his cheeks.....who's a cheeky little sausage? You never hear her suddenly blurt out, ' and who's got a lovely big dick then?'

Being a new kid on the block, I would often be invited to various functions by patrons of the shop and it wasn't long before we built up a circle of friends. Obviously, having young children to consider, our social life was mainly a case of inviting people round for drinks and a few nibbles. (I love that expression - it sounds so 'correct'. So much better than a couple of beers and a cheese and pickle sandwich).

Sadly, the marriage revival was short lived! I discovered that my wife was having an affair with a local fire fighter. He and his wife were part of our social circle. As such, he would often put his arm round me and say 'how's it going mate?', but somehow always stopping short of saying, Oh, yeah, by the way, I'm shagging your missus!

He was twice the size of me and it would probably have represented a death wish on my part to take a swing at him. However, what I ended up doing, gave me more satisfaction that I could ever have imagined.

The fire station would often have open days, where the public could walk around the fire engines and chat to the fire fighters. Some of the wives would go along with their children to show them what daddy got up to when he wasn't at home giving them piggy back rides. On one such day, I mingled with the crowd and a couple of brigade top brass. Several people had told me what was going on and I knew that Yvette had told him that they had been rumbled. He probably figured that I would be too scared to do anything about it. So imagine the look on his face when I walked up to him. The fire fighters were being asked all sorts of questions such as, 'is it exciting driving fast in a fire engine?' 'Do you get frightened when you see the flames leaping all around you?' So imagine his expression when, in front of his wife and about fifty other people I asked him out loud, 'is it exciting shagging another man's wife while he is out working hard to pay the bills? Is it also easy to forget your own wife and children when you are screwing another woman behind their backs?'

Needless to say, I was on the verge of being escorted from the premises when I turned and walked away. As I looked round to take one last glance at the arsehole, his wife had already shouted something at him and was walking away with the kids. I figured that my wife would be getting a visit from her sooner or later and from the look on her face, I didn't think it would be just to enquire as to whether or not she had enjoyed it. I also had to consider the likelihood of walking round a corner one dark night and getting my head kicked in, but I never heard another word!

Three years later there was to be a tragic sequel to that little episode. I heard through the grapevine that the guy in question had died of cancer. I'm not sure, but I don't think he made it to forty years of age. Fate moves in mysterious ways.

A couple of weeks after hearing about the guy dying, David was in the area and came to have lunch with me. When I told him the news, his first reaction was, 'fucking hell! That's a result innit?' But I could not feel that way, I would not have wished that upon him. What he did was wrong, but it takes two to tango! After I explained that to David, he shrugged his shoulders and said. 'Yeah, I guess you're right bruv....it's hard to be a Christian sometimes and do what's right'.

Chapter eight: A brush with the heavies

Within a year, I had the Gillingham shop running like a well oiled machine and had made friends with a man who was a bookmaking legend in Kent. His name was John 'Curly' Wilson. We had met up a couple of times at charity fund raising events and I had become aware that this was what I wanted out of life. To be in a position to help some of the unfortunate souls that were cropping up in our newspapers and on television. Little did I know what lay ahead!

Curly, very quickly became my hero and has been one of the most influential people to come into my life. He was everything that I wanted to be!

Among his many business interest, Curley had a betting shop in Queenborough on the Isle of Sheppey. He was also involved with Dumpton Park dog racing stadium at Ramsgate. He took one look at my CV and said straight away that I should be running my own shop. This had been a dream of mine for some time but I didn't have the capital. Also, it was a very nerve racking prospect if you think about it. I was thirty years old, had a wife and two children plus a mortgage and ran a car. All of my betting shop experience to date revolved around playing with someone else's money. My Mecca wages were there every month. Irrelevant of profit margins, property cost, staff wages, cleaner, corporation tax and insurance, C I S fees and much more. It was a big step to take! Oh, yes there was something else. I didn't have the money.

What happened next was a true measure of the man who later admitted that he virtually looked upon me as a son. He invited me to dinner one evening and put a proposal on the table which knocked me sideways. Curly knew that I desperately wanted to get into the betting shop industry but that I was reluctant to take the gamble, if you'll excuse the pun! He made me an offer that I could not refuse and I think that I would be right in saying that you would have to search hard to find a similar offer on the open market.

He would sell me the Queenborough shop for nine thousand pounds. He would do all the necessary to help me get the C I S license and add up the cost of all the other various bits and pieces required to get started. If, at any time in the first year, for any reason at all, I was not happy about things. He would refund every penny spent and buy the shop back off me for what I had paid him.

I discussed it with Yvette and was amazed to find that, not only was she totally supportive, she even got her father to loan me the nine grand. I spoke to a solicitor who subsequently drew up the contracts. We both signed and Curly cracked open a bottle of champagne. It was 1982 and I had been in the betting industry for ten years, working for Mecca. Now I had my own betting shop....I was IT.

The shop was well established and Curly spent the first week introducing me to his regular customers His regular board man, Sam, and a young female assistant named Gabby 'came with the shop', so to speak. I was quite happy to continue with them. I would normally arrive at the shop between 8.30am and 9.00am and have the papers up on the wall and kettle on by the time the girl arrived at 10.00am.

I was earning a steady wage and working sensible hours (Sunday racing and night meetings hadn't arrived at this point in time). The driving backwards and forwards to Gillingham each day was a bit of a drag, but I was into a steady routine and spending more quality time with the family........things were looking up!   The sun was shining and life was great! Everything I had ever dreamed about was coming true, what could possibly happen to spoil it?.........Plenty!!

As mentioned, I was living in Gillingham when I bought the shop on Sheppey. Two more weeks with Mecca and I was going to be my own boss. I used to have a quick pint at the end of the day in a pub near the Gillingham shop. On the day we signed the contracts for my new shop, I had a couple more pints than usual and got talking to a couple of guys from out of town. I told them about my new shop on Sheppey and insisted that they pop in and see me some time. They wished me luck and promised to pop in and see me if they were ever in that neck of the woods.

Four weeks after opening up my very own betting shop in Queenborough, the door opened around lunchtime one Friday and in walked the two guys plus a friend. They greeted me like a long lost cousin and invited me to go next door into The

Phillippa to have a drink with them. I was covered by the till girl Gabby and my board man. Racing didn't start for another half hour, so I agreed to join them in the pub for a quick one.

When I walked into the pub, the three men were sitting at a table over in the corner and had already got me a pint of lager. I sat down and explained that I didn't have long and had to be back in time for the first race.

They started telling me about a guy they knew who had started up a betting business in London and had been having a run of bad luck. Apparently the shop had been broken into twice and someone had squirted petrol through the letter box one night and had left a note saying 'next time we light it!' They started to say that there were some despicable people around, but I twigged what their game was and knew what was coming.

I took a tenner out of my pocket as I stood up and said, 'get another round of drinks in while I make sure everything's okay in the shop,' and walked away.

I went into the shop and phoned the police. They gave me instructions.

'Keep them talking in the pub and we will get there as quickly as possible. We need to hear one of them threaten you before we can arrest them, so we will be hiding in the shop when you all walk back in.'

I told the staff what was happening and got myself back into the pub before they could come looking for me. I told the girl to come and get me as soon as it was all set up. I knew that I had to stay calm, but needless to say, my arse was twitching and my heart was pounding as I walked back into the bar.

Luckily, up to the point where I walked out, they hadn't said enough to indicate their intentions, so they had no reason to think that I had already twigged what they were after.

As soon as I sat down, the ring leader carried on where he'd left off. He launched into a story about a mate of theirs who had been through a similar experience as the one that they were outlining to me. He wouldn't let me get a word in edgeways and was saying things like, 'they murdered his cat......put sugar in his petrol tank.......crapped on his doorstep'.......anything to keep the conversation going. I was just praising the three guys for being kind enough to warn me about the despicable scumbags that do that sort of thing and how lucky I was to have mates like them. Suddenly, my till girl came walking into the pub and said, 'Barry, you are wanted on the phone.'

I stood up and started to walk away, but one of the guys put his hand on my shoulder. 'But Barry, we haven't told you the best part yet, we've had this really brilliant idea regarding you and your shop. It's all about insurance and we think that you will find it very interesting especially the outcome of it all.'

Strangely enough, listening to him prattling away for ten minutes and knowing what I knew, I had relaxed somewhat and felt more in control of the situation.

'Ah! don't tell me he found out who was doing it all and got a gun and shot them! Here, come back into the shop and have a coffee before you go, while I find out who's on the phone.'

Before they could reply, I was out of the pub door and almost running into the betting shop. I had managed to get behind my counter before the three guys came walking in again. They strolled over to the counter and glared at the till girl. Then at my board man, who was an old timer but as streetwise as they come. There were no punters in the shop at the time. The mouthy one looked at me and shook his head.

'I don't think you realise what's happening here sunshine! The bottom line is this. You pay us a percentage of your weekly profits and you get to stay in business. We don't need to touch you, Barry, because if two or three of your punters get thumped while they're having a bet, they won't want to come in here anymore....if you get my drift? And that's only for starters mate! We'll find out where you live and what school your kids go to. Do you get my drift?'

Before I could say a word, two police officers stepped out from the office behind me. As the three guys turned to run, they were faced with two more uniformed officers standing in the shop doorway.

They were arrested and cautioned and taken outside in handcuffs.

The police searched their car and laid down the law concerning, 'demanding money with menaces'. At the same time, they were searching via Criminal Records Dept to see if there was anything known.

The outcome was that the guys were detained, photographed and released with a caution that if they set foot on the island again they would be arrested. I was asked if I wanted to press charges. I confirmed that, as long as the incident remained on record and they never attempted to contact me again, I would be happy for the police to handle it as they saw fit.

Amazing isn't it? I worked for Mecca for ten years with nothing worse than an irate loser to contend with, but after four weeks of running my own shop, I got a visit from a gang of muscle brains wanting a partnership in my business!

In 1984 we sold the house in Gillingham and bought a three bed semi enjoying South facing garden laid to lawn with garage and rear entrance. It was situated in Queenborough......about ten minutes walk from the shop......and 'The Queen Phillippa' pub.

The Phillippa was full of characters with some great stories to tell about the island and the people living there, it had became my local since buying the shop.

In between setting up the shop in the morning and the start of afternoon racing, my lunch would more often than not, consist of a pie and a pint. (No woman for the night).

Most of my business would be conducted in The Phillippa and it was almost my second home. In fact there were some locals who thought that I lived there and just popped next door occasionally to put a bet on!

One Saturday after closing the shop, I walked into the pub for a well earned pint. There was a good crowd building up that summer's evening and I was soon in the midst of it. Two games of pool, three games of darts and a Chas & Dave sing along with the football team.

Several 'well earned pints' later, I suddenly remembered, to my horror, that my wife had told me over breakfast, that she was going to a club with some friends that evening and was being picked up by a taxi at 10pm. It was now 10.45pm and I had a ten minute walk ahead of me.....ooops!

Needless to say, I was greeted with a barrage of abuse. Words which put a question mark over my birthright preceded by the word 'selfish' for example. Also, being likened to the crude name often used as an alternative to the orifice in one's, 'bottom'......it was all par for the course.

Saying, 'I'm sorry....I will make it up to you,' was a pointless exercise and a waste of breath. As was offering ten pounds for her to buy a couple of bottles of wine to share with her friends. This particular peace offering attracted another reference to the orifice in one's bottom as a suggested location for the ten pound note and the wine bottles. Apart from the pain of such actions, I could never treat wine with such disrespect.

After enduring ten minutes of ear bashing and door slamming, the re-ordered taxi pulled away and it was peaceful once again.

Now! A well educated person with an open mind would have seen both sides of the argument. Probably touching on various aspects of selfishness, sexism, human rights and political correctness and rounding off with a reminder about ' playing the game'. All of which would be would be perfectly acceptable and in order.

The following morning, during a telephone conversation with brother David, I told him about the incident. This was his assessment of the situation and his advice on the appropriate action to take.

'Listen bruv! You work your bollocks off all week earning a big enough wedge to put the bacon on the table. You pay the bills, feed her and the kids and give her money to go clubbing. She should fall down on her knees and kiss your feet, mate. Do yourself a favour, if she climbs in bed tonight, feeling a bit frisky and starts having a reef round the meat and two vedge, push her away and tell her she aint getting it until she learns some fuckin' respect'.

Absolutely priceless isn't it? I can't remember which university **he** went to! ha ha.

David doesn't actually talk like that all the time, but he will occasionally put it on, just for effect. As indeed Ronnie Barker did when playing Fletcher in Porridge! If I think about it, I suppose that makes me young Godber!

The shop turned out to be a good move and I was soon making a nice steady living out of it. The children were settled into their new schools and life looked quite promising. There was an element of sadness on its way though!

In 1985, my daughter Chantelle came home from school one day with tears in her eyes and told us that her friend had been diagnosed with Leukaemia. The little girl's name was Rosie Miller.

As parents of young children, we were aware of 'there but for the grace of God'.

I had been thinking out loud about charitable causes for some time. My thoughts had been triggered off by a recent conversation that I'd had with Curly Wilson. He said that he was involved with a couple of charity organisations and described the thoughts and pleasure that he got from helping people less fortunate than ourselves. Curly made me aware that the suffering and pain they were going through could be alleviated somewhat by giving them something exciting to look forward to.

I phoned Curly and asked for his advice on how to get started on raising money to help Rosie and her family. That conversation was to be the turning point in my life.

As Curly began to describe the various ways to raise funds, my mind was racing ahead. I found myself coming up with ideas of my own and even at that early moment in time I was feeling the exhilaration and the adrenalin caused by the thought that I was about to do something really worthwhile. If I'm honest, I was probably experiencing the first really unselfish moment of my life so far!

The die was cast, I was motivated!

During the next eighteen months, by way of raffles, collections and begging letters I raised £5,000! Thirty years ago, that was probably the equivalent of £30,000 at today's prices.

The five grand, which included £1000 spending money, was given to Rosie and her family. It enabled them to fly to Orlando for a week and stay in Disneyland. I cannot describe the feelings of happiness and satisfaction it gave me to see the little girl's face as they broke the news to her. I stood there and imagined my father was watching the event and promised him that this was just the beginning. I had found my true purpose in life. Although I was unaware of it at the time, my efforts had not gone unnoticed by a couple of people who were to become major figures in my life for quite a few years to come.

I heard that Rosie and her family had a wonderful time in America and were treated like royalty. Sadly, Rosie passed away in 2014. I hope that the public awareness created by the 'Disneyland' article in the newspapers all those years ago, would have encouraged others to think about similar cases and make them want to help out in some small way. No other feeling that I have experienced can possibly compare with the satisfaction one feels when bringing comfort and happiness into a sick child's life.

Top: With Pat Jennings and one hand on the F.A. Cup
Bottom: "Bagsy" morning exercise. Sadly, he never won the Grand
National!

During the making of the Fools and Horses episode *'Jolly Boys Outing',* I was given the job of entertaining David Jason, Buster Merrifield and Nicholas Lyndhurst, along with other members of the cast, for three days. The Dumpton Park Stadium car park was used as a set for the market scenes and Palm Bay car park was where they blew the coach up. Wonderful memories for me and my children!

MAY 2, 2002

Barry Coombs with some of the children who will be going on a Jubilee holiday   2/656/22)

CHILDREN from Hill Crest Home in High Road, Leytonstone, are off on a summer holiday thanks to the people at William Hill.

The bookies donated enough cash to send seven disadvantaged children, aged between 12 and 14, to Butlins in Bognor Regis.

The kids and five adult carers will enjoy a week's half board at the holiday centre in Jubilee Week in June, with all expenses paid. Butlin's also granted a 50 per cent discount for the group.

Barry Coombs, a senior manager at William Hill, surprised the children on Saturday when he presented them with the details of their holiday.

Top: Some of the lucky children who went to Butlins.
Bottom: 3 years fund raising for Wish Upon a Star.

Two very special moments in one! Spending time with the great man himself. One of nature's true gentlemen, Bob Champion.
Sharing the launching of Tommo's (Derek Thompson) autobiography. A great guy to be with, Tommo shares my sense of humour.
All three of us have one thing in common - surviving cancer!

 *William* **HILL**

Invite you to meet Channel 4 Racing's **John Francome and Derek Thompson**
at the launch of their new look
William Hill, adjacent to The House of Fraser
FRIDAY 2nd DECEMBER 1994 AT 12 noon

Above Left: With my original Mecca Area Manager, Bob Williams. Above Right: Gordon Campbell OBE. He truly inspired me during my cancer period in hospital Bottom: Tommo and top flat racing jockey, Richard Fox. (love that face!)

Me and 'Arry' with 'The Minitones' - Kenny Baker and Jack Purvis. They were in the Star Wars films. Kenny was inside R2-D2.

'The Winkle Trio!' Tony Cook, Barry Coombs and John (Arry) McCloud. Tony was my chauffeur, minder and wet nurse. Over the years, he probably put me to bed more times than my mum did when I was a baby. After a good night out on the juice, it was like a scene from the film 'Arthur', as Tony opened the car door, I would fall out into the road, laughing. (Happy Days!).

Thank you messages from Brenda Blethryn and Frank Bruno. Along with so
many other celebrities they work tirelessly to help good causes.

Seven annual Gala Night's at Walthamstow Stadium, raised £80,000-00 for
Waltham Forest NHS and over £15,000-00 for Wish Upon A Star.

My son, Ben (the white one) with "The Sheppey Zulus". They raise money for worthy causes at various Charity events on the Island.

Well! I must have done something good. A sunny day in London with the new love of my life, Wing Man. At long last I did it right.

Chapter nine: France or bust

Meanwhile, back in the shop. One little scheme that I had incorporated into my business was 'Telephone Betting'. This was something that the big shops were somewhat wary of at the time because it was wide open to abuse. I was made aware that people would often fancy a bet whilst at work and couldn't get away to put it on..... well what are friends for?

Having made sure that the punters who wanted that facility were credit worthy, I got them to sign an undertaking. Also, I gave them a unique password. I imposed a maximum limit, in case one of the staff accidentally accepted a bet that could hurt me. Telephone punters had to have sufficient funds in their account to cover all bets. I also had the facility to lay off a big bet with one of the top shops if need be. The last thing a small shop needs is some lucky punter getting all five up in a pound win Canadian with a couple of 20/1 shots in it. I know I said it was a good advert for the big boys but it could be the kiss of death for a small shop if the manager didn't lay it off in time.

When Curly saw how well the telephone betting was doing, he suggested that I should extend that facility to the island's caravan holiday sites at Leysdown.

After several visits to the camps and a couple of the local pubs, I was able to set up a betting arrangement with the site management. Telephone betting was gaining in popularity but was still in its infancy. I had quickly become aware of its potential and it transpires that what I was doing was in fact the forerunner of today's telephone and online betting craze.

It was whilst building up the camp and pub connections that I became aware of something very interesting! Something that was to become another major episode and have a massive effect on my life.

I realised that there were hardly any sea food stalls around. You couldn't get a winkle or a shrimp for love nor money. A sight that was common in London was virtually nonexistent less than fifty miles down the road. As far as I was concerned, seafood stalls and pubs made **great** bedfellows but at this moment in time they were as rare as the proverbial 'rocking horse poo'!

As mentioned earlier, I was a great lover of sea food. David explained that this was probably genetic, courtesy of mum's brother, Percy Charles, being a seafood vendor.

I think David based his theory on the fact that he had developed natural tradesman skills and followed our father into the building game. That's after he'd established that he and his band were not going to be the next Beatles or Rolling Stones. As David so eloquently put it a few years later, as part of an after dinner speech. 'Being part of a band in the sixties was fun......you got to see the world, got ripped off, learned how it felt to go hungry, screwed a few birds and ended up having to face the reality of, 'you aint going nowhere mate'. No identity, no imagination, all we ever did was play other people's poxy songs.' Several years later, he abbreviated that appraisal to, 'it was a total waste of time and energy!'

Exactly where David learned to speak in such eloquent tones is still a mystery!

Over the years he developed his building business, incorporating a timber and damp treatment service along the way. Upon securing his surveyor's qualifications he expanded into specialist consultancy and became a respected figure in diagnostic appraisal of structural fatigue due to damp and timber infestation. He enjoyed a good lifestyle for many years, before selling up and retiring to become a full time writer. I think it was obvious to everyone, that because of his way with words and his obvious grasping of the English language it was only a question of time!

I found and rented a small lock up unit, five minutes away in Sheerness and set about converting it to a sea food preparation unit. By the time I'd finished, it boasted refrigeration, hot and cold running water and cooking facilities.

The unit was subsequently inspected and passed by the health authorities and I was up and running........or as David put it.......'just like uncle Percy bruv........stuff me!   It's bloody genetic mate........that's what it is'!

Ha, ha it's sheer poetry isn't it?

Those caravan camps were full of Londoners and following my chat with the owners, I let it be known that Barry Coombs' sea food services would soon be available. It had been a dream of mine for many years, but like so many dreams, I had begun to think that it was just another one of the 'daytime' variety.

The sea food services took off fast and furious....I had got my sums right on this one!

I often look back on that period of my life and remember how exciting it all was. My only regret at the time was my wife's reluctance to get involved. If nothing else it would have meant us seeing a lot more of each other......I wouldn't have spent so much time in the pubs......drinking and laughing......being greeted by a load of smiling faces calling, 'here he comes.....Mr cockles and mussels alive alive-O! Come to think of it.......she probably wouldn't have enjoyed it at all........yeah! I think it was probably for the best that she didn't get involved!........miserable bitch.

My wife liked it on the island and we quickly developed a social circle. As far as I'm concerned, God in his infinite wisdom gave us warm summer evenings so that we could have friends round for Bar-B-Qs and cold beer. Yvette and I both realised that this was our last chance to make the marriage work.

The kids were at full time school and I thought that it was a good time for my wife to get involved in the family business and help out. Sadly, she wasn't interested in becoming a 'fishwife' as she put it, so it was still, all down to me. Strange isn't it, but when I look back on life it seems that it was always, 'all down to me'.

My problem was, I could never walk away from a business opportunity and this would often mean socialising after work. I don't think there was ever a time when I wasn't involved in some kind of venture.

I soon had five staff going out with baskets of prawns, cockles and mussels, crab sticks etc, every Friday, Saturday and Sunday. They covered the camps and pubs on the island and always came back with empty baskets, luvely jubbly!

I would sometimes carry an extra basket if there was a do on at the pub. One guy asked my girl if he could have a whole crab. Across a crowded pub on a Saturday night she shouted. 'Barry, have you got crabs?' Quick as a flash I replied, 'no, my pants are a bit tight.' The place erupted!

Up at 4.30am and on my way to Billingsgate market three times a week and sometimes buying from local fishermen, my stuff was always fresh. Quite often, on returning from Billingsgate, I would put in a couple of hours at the preparation unit before opening up the betting shop. The cooking smell coming from the unit was intoxicating at times and people would often knock on the door and purchase bowls of various delicious morsels. Cockles and mussels for breakfast, now there's a thought.

Once cooked, the seafood would be chilled down and distributed to the various outlets and sold on the same day.

'What about jellied eels?' I hear you say.

Jellied eels were very expensive to buy! The choice from the suppliers was £8 for a tub of 'tail ends', £10 for 'tail and middle', £13 for 'all middle'. A tub would do 12 portions and I only bought 'tail and middle' and 'all middle' tubs, so at £1.20 per portion, jellied eels was virtually a loss leader.

Once in a while I would be asked to cater for a club evening or some kind of celebration. This I enjoyed, because it meant that monsieur Barry, the 'chef de cuisine' could come into action. I would cook and prepare on the premises and treat the guests to my 'piece de resistance' which was mussels cooked in garlic and cream with a splash of white wine. Also, if **they** wanted to splash out, they could follow up with a crab cocktail served in the shell. In Henry the Eighth's days, both these dishes were said to have aphrodisiac affects! That wouldn't surprise me....they was a dirty bunch of sods those Tudors!........mussel madness. Their motto was, 'stick it where the crabsticks!'

Chatting to David one day, I was telling him how things were getting really busy and that our popularity was growing. He suggested creating an image that would be our own personal trademark. Something like a distinguishable jacket or a funny hat!

I mentioned the possibility of 'overkill' and related a 'fable' that I had heard on TV a short while before. A comedian was saying to the audience.   'Aren't people strange sometimes? They can see a man playing the guitar and harmonica at the same time and say, 'that man's a genius!' But, if he straps a drum on his back and cymbals on his knees, they are more inclined to cross over the road and pretend they haven't seen him!

David smiled and said, 'so a white bowler hat with, 'I've Got Crabs Round My Winkle' written across the front, is out then?'

'Afraid so,' I laughed.

Travelling back and forth to London and Sheppey each day; running a sea food business and a betting shop....I never had time to be bored, but sadly, my wife did! The relationship was stretched to breaking point. Both children were at full time school and there was no reason why she couldn't have done a few hours each day helping out in the seafood business. I would have been able to put her on the payroll and she could have run the preparation unit. I was later to learn that this would have interfered with her social life!

Whilst the betting office and the seafood projects were building up more business, I was building up a healthy appetite. Gabby would cover for me whilst I popped into the cafe next door for a brunch, or sometimes a sandwich and a pint in the pub. This gave me the opportunity to catch up on all the local gossip.

It was on one such occasion in 1986 that I heard the news that a group of mates were creeping over to France for the weekend to watch the French Derby at Chantilly Racecourse. It featured a horse called 'Bering' which was trained in France by Criquette Head and being ridden on the day by top jockey in England at that time, Gary Moore. Reports indicated that the horse was flying on the home gallops and I had been putting a few quid on it at various prices, the best being 2/1.

We had company coming to stay that weekend and I knew that my missus would not agree to me shooting over to France for two days. I had an idea and phoned Chris, the husband. As we discussed the coming event I casually slipped into the conversation, 'don't forget to bring your passport.' It went quiet for two seconds then he spluttered, 'but I don't need a passport to get onto the Isle of Sheppey, or have you renounced your sovereignty and become a republic since we were there at Easter. I couldn't go into all the details on the phone, so I repeated, 'just bring it, Chris, I'll explain when you get here.'

After racing had finished on that Saturday afternoon in June, I went home to find that our visitors had arrived. I just had time for a quick cup of tea and a sandwich before suggesting that I took Chris down the pub for a pint. The girls were having a bit of a chinwag and preparing dinner so it was a half hearted gesture as they said, 'goodbye, see you later'.

I had put an overnight bag in the car earlier that day so I told Chris to make sure that he had a topcoat and his passport with him. We laughed as we drove off and Chris reminded me that all he had to wear was the clothes he stood up in. In fact, his wife hadn't even opened their suitcase yet so his clothes hadn't been unpacked.

I pointed out that it wouldn't have made a blind bit of difference if they had been. After all, as far as the girls were concerned, we were popping up the road for a quick pint. There was no way that he could have justifies taking clean shirt, socks and pants with him! Even I'm not that good!

We arrived at Dover and parked up. We boarded the Boulogne ferry and went straight into the bar. 'I wonder if there's a phone on the ship?' asked Chris, 'I must ring and say to her, 'you're not to worry about anything darling. We're just going to France for a couple of days and I'll bring you something nice home!'

I was rummaging around in my overnight grip and looked at him in amazement, 'you are having me on aren't you? They're not going laugh this one off mate. We are condemned men...enjoy it while you can. What size pants are you? '

I could see that this was Chris's first 'naughty boy' adventure and I couldn't help reflecting on what a bad influence I was. As it turned out, there was a bit of a heat wave on and the girls spent two days sunbathing and drinking wine in the back garden. They already knew where we were because when they'd gone looking for us in The Phillippa at ten o'clock that night, the whole pub cheered and started singing, 'They're on their way to sunny France, to see the French Derby!' (to the tune of Viva Espania).

We made our way to Amiens station and met up with another Chris. He was carrying a crate of champagne which I had won off him merely by turning up. He had bet me that I wouldn't have the balls to do it. As we popped opened a bottle of Laurent, I explained that it would only be after I returned home that I would have to worry about my balls.....but this would help to numb the pain!....cheers! We opened two more bottles of Champagne and shared them with our fellow French passengers. We had the happiest carriage on the train and stepped off at Chantilly doing a conga!

What a great day at Chantilly! Bering won the Derby in a new record time and I had won £500. (Probably the equivalent of three grand today). We got legless and I don't even remember going to bed.

I do, however remember returning home at lunchtime on Monday.....it was so difficult to wipe the stupid smiles off our faces. We just held our hands up and sat there like a couple of naughty schoolboys!.

Chris's wife wasn't too bad and even smiled a couple of times. I still think that it was a good job that he had their car keys in his pocket though. My little angel on the other hand, not noted for her sense of humour, I had to buy her off. It cost me a new dress, shoes and handbag and a table for two but apart from a couple of snide comments, it went much better than expected and my testicles were safe for a little longer!

Chapter ten: Not enough hours

I mentioned John 'Curly' Wilson earlier and how he had influenced my fund raising activities. John had a 'pitch' at Dumpton Park greyhound stadium in Ramsgate. As mentioned, he was an ardent supporter of worthy causes and had been raising money to purchase a laser machine for Margate hospital.

Among other functions this machine could carry out operations on women with cervical cancer as an alternative to 'open surgery' and had been highly acclaimed in the medical journals.

The target for the purchase of this 'miracle of modern science' was £35,000. (£150,000 at today's prices). Curly was running out of ideas and had heard about my success with the Rosie Miller project. He asked Sheila Yandle, who was top manager at Dumpton for 26 years, if he could invite me along to Dumpton to put fresh life and some new ideas into the 'Laser Machine Fund Raising' scheme.

I accepted the challenge and took to the task like a fish to water. It was a piece of cake! I mean just think about it. Me and my helpers waving our buckets on one side of the turnstile and two thousand holiday makers with their pockets bulging queuing to get in on the other.

They never knew what hit them....poor sods!

As they were handed their programmes, gone was the traditional, 'good evening, have a nice time and good luck'. They were shown some harrowing pictures and given a short lecture on cervical cancer, along with the parting comment, 'just think of these poor souls, next time you are sitting on the beach licking your cornet!...... Have a nice holiday!

We reached the target within a year!

The laws regarding human rights hadn't been abused at that time and all this cobblers about things being 'politically correct' hadn't even been thought of. We still had our Christian values, supported 100% by democracy and freedom of speech. We were allowed to let our conscience be our guide.

The management at Margate Hospital were gobsmacked when they saw what we had done for them and once again the media made the most of it. Hopefully it was an indication to others as to what can be achieved if you put your mind to it. Shame on the government for not funding the NHS better.

This was the period in time that the Channel tunnel was in progress and I had been watching with interest the rapid development of a project called 'Farthinglow Village'. It was an ever growing collection of portable cabins and mobile homes which housed the various tradesmen and labour force involved in the latest invasion of France. There was one building in particular that really interested me though, a new clubhouse.

The project was being run by Kelvin International Ltd. I was introduced to the site manager, Kieran White and the bar manager, Bob

McPhearson. With their help and approval I was to organise cabaret and race nights over the next three years. Also, I set up a telephone betting service for the benefit of the work force.

I was to develop a really good relationship with Bob. He was very streetwise and had a great sense of humour. He also had the keys to the directors' drink cabinet, so we were virtually joined at the hip for three years.

That brings me to another critical moment in my entrepreneurial period.

Because of my new found celebrity lifestyle, I was being offered free drinks all the time. You would have to tape my mouth up and strap my arms to my side to stop me saying 'yes please', but with drink driving being clamped down on I had to make a decision whether to pack up drinking or driving. That was another no contest. I got myself a chauffeur, actually it was more than that.

Due to increased activity at the Channel Tunnel club and the sea food business expanding, I was often being called upon to carry large amounts of money for wages and suchlike. Well Mike Tyson I am not.

My minder/driver came in the shape of Tony Cook. 6'2" tall weighing in at 15 stone. Craggy faced and streetwise. For the next three years he would drive me around, watch my back and on several occasions.......put me to bed.

It was often thought, especially by David, that the film 'Arthur' starring Dudley Moore, was based on my lifestyle during that period. The number of times I tumbled out of a car into the road laughing my head off, only served to endorse the wisdom of my decision not to drive. It was the kind of scenario that traffic cops would dream about! At the height of a good evening I could do a perfect impression of Freddie Frinton. (That will test your memory). He played the best and funniest drunk on TV and in films years ago.

As you are probably becoming aware, I was cramming more and more challenges and commitments into life and desperately needed someone to rearrange the clock in order to create a thirty hour day.

I had always enjoyed spending time with my children but I was seeing less of them these days due to them often being in bed asleep by the time I arrived home. Ben, who was coming up to nine years old, would often accompany me on my Sunday morning rounds, selling sea food in a few pubs on the island. It was a confidence building exercise for him and he was very popular with the punters.

Ben was artistically gifted and would often draw some fascinating pictures. Most of his work was of the futuristic variety and I will openly admit to not always knowing if I was holding it the right way up! But it was fascinating stuff alright and I was proud of his attitude towards life. It was thanks to my son that I came to realise that a 'transformer' was not necessarily a voltage regulator! On the contrary, it would often have the strength of ten men. I wished I did sometimes!'

Ben went on to serve an apprenticeship and today he is a successful electrician.

He has a wife Carly, son Callum and daughter Courtney and is a devoted father. His son Callum is a good footballer and plays for a local team.

Ben is now 37 and helps to run a group of local businessmen known as 'The Sheppey Zulus'. They dress up and organise various fund raising events to help support worthy causes on the Isle of Sheppey. (David's genetic theory kicking in again, like father like son!). At Ben's request, I recently organised a charity race night for The Sheppey Zulus and helped them raise £600. In one of the photos in the picture section of this book, you will see the Zulus. Ben is the corporal.

It was good to meet so many of my son's friends and colleagues. They are a great crowd and we had a wonderful evening. They posted a thank you on Twitter a few days later and I printed it off as a keepsake. I guess I'm still a bit traditional in my attitude towards this ever changing world, but a small show of gratitude makes it all worthwhile and goes a long way with me.

I was now getting quite involved with various activities at Dumpton Park and Sheila Yandell asked me if I would be interested in becoming a summer cover manager. The job entailed looking after the restaurant and night club during the holiday season.

I was running regular charity night race meetings and several celebrities graced the events with their presence. Neal Foulds, the snooker professional owned dogs that sometimes ran at Dumpton.

I was constantly on the lookout for 'worthy causes', so taking on the job at Dumpton Park enabled me to keep my finger on the pulse. Also, it became a good venue to meet and entertain my business colleagues and fellow fund raisers.

One such get together resulted in my becoming aware of a group of children who were suffering from life threatening and terminal illnesses.

There were twelve children in all and £300 per child was required to send them on a pilgrimage to Lourdes in France. Within a few weeks I had raised the £3,600 needed to send them on their journey of hope. It was very moving to think that, sadly, some of them would not be making any such future journeys. I find it quite harrowing at times and never cease to admire the wonderful people who have dedicated their whole life to helping seriously ill children

Things were going well at the Tunnel and 'Kelvin International' were very pleased with my services. There were plenty of things going on at the club, so the lads working there were always looking forward to one event or another.

Bob McPhearson and Kieran White became very supportive of my fund raising efforts and I owe them a big thank you for their contributions. They and a few of the lads became regulars at Dumpton Park, not only to have a drink and a flutter but to become involved in sponsoring various fund raising events. They were responsible on many occasions for getting people to sponsor races on the programme and they encouraged other business outlets to follow suit.

I was now struggling to cover all my commitments and decided to take on a partner in the seafood business.

Since moving onto the island, I had gradually become good friends with a taxi driver named John McCloud. He was a 'thinking man' and very thoughtful. I thought a lot of him and think he knew I thought that way. Thinking back, I thought very carefully before asking him if he'd ever thought of becoming a partner in my seafood business!! He said he'd been thinking about it and thought he'd wait until I asked. That's very wise don't you think?

I took him down the bank and had his name put on the Barry Coombs Seafood ownership. It proved to be a good move and his presence halved my load. It gave me the breathing space I needed and 25% discount on all future taxi journeys!

It is surprising how many people, when first approached to help out in an appeal, just shake their heads and say, 'sorry I'm really not interested.....don't have the time!' It doesn't end there of course and three months later I find them thanking me for allowing them to be a part of something very special.

 Their initial reaction is par for the course. Let's face it, how many people include in their list of, 'things to do today.' must help a sick child?

I once saw a fifteen stone rugby player reduced to tears, when I handed him a card from a seven year old girl who wrote saying, 'thank you all for helping me!' As we walked out of the hospital, he turned and said, 'that was probably the most worthwhile thing I have ever done in my entire life.'

My nickname for John McCloud was 'Arry'. He was the perfect choice and did a grand job. John was totally self motivating and never bothered me unless it was absolutely essential.

Tony Cook was now with me full time. On top of his other duties, I had him selling and transporting seafood. It was extra money and much better than standing around waiting for me all the time. When I told him he had to wear white shirt and trousers and a yellow bow tie, he flinched and said, 'I hope I don't bump into anyone I know.' 'Arry told him that he looked 'cute' and quickly ducked! 'Arry had a great sense of humour and would start singing, 'me and my shadow,' when Tony and I walked into the room.

Chapter eleven: Last family Christmas

God moves in mysterious ways and fate often takes a hand. I was becoming more and more concerned about not being able to spend as much time in the betting shop as I should. I guess I must have said something along the way, because out of the blue, I had an offer from one of my biggest regular punters who wanted to buy into the business.

Allan Milton was a local entrepreneur who owned a big house and drove a Rolls Royce. Apart from being a really great guy he was also a high roller and I was constantly on my guard whenever he came in for a bet. He was the only regular punter that could hurt me financially if I wasn't careful. He would often put a big lump on a horse. I would study the bet and if I was nervous, I would lay as much as 80% of it off with the big boys and I have to admit to breaking into a sweat a couple of times when he had the second part of a big double running on.

I drank with Allan a few times and he knew that I was being stretched to almost breaking point by my commitments. I said 'yes' to his offer and set about getting him registered as a bookmaker in his own right. When it finally came through, he was over the moon.

It suited me to have partners in my businesses because it gave me the freedom to move around and do a few deals. Trouble was brewing on the home front though!

I was never at home these days and my family life was suffering because of it. Looking back, if I'm honest, I can't say that I was surprised to hear one or two stories about my wife. She was very attractive, and was bored out of her mind.

She was being left on her own for too many long periods and there were plenty of lads around who wanted to keep her company.

Christmas 1986 was bad and if it hadn't been for David coming to stay with us, we probably wouldn't have celebrated Christmas at all.

David had just divorced his second wife and had taken the pledge. 'Women? Never again!' He had been through an emotional roller coaster trying to make his marriage work with a woman he later described as a 'piece of shit'. Not one to beat about the bush is our David!

Following advice from a work colleague, David bought some equipment and tapped his own phone. When he played back the tapes it was as he suspected, his wife was having affairs and he recognised a couple of the men involved. The latest one was with a young boy she worked with in the evenings at the local telephone exchange.

She was despised by her workmates who knew of her despicable behaviour. They also knew David to be a good husband and devoted father. David could have torn the youngster apart but decided that this time it was the camels straw and decided to call it a day. As David confronted the poor trembling bastard he told him, 'You've got no idea what you're letting yourself in for, pal. I've just wasted some of the best years of my life on that arsehole, now it's your turn! Welcome to Hell.

She had a child by the boy and married him a year or so later. She never changed her ways and subjected him to absolute hell on earth. He divorced her a few years later.

The last he heard she'd married some rich prick. 'Poor bastard,' said David, she's probably convinced him that she's a vestal virgin.'

Not long after his split, we invited David to spend Christmas with us so as to cheer him up. It turned out to be the other way round. As I said, if it hadn't been for him, we probably wouldn't have celebrated Christmas at all that year.

He arrived at 9.30 am on Christmas morning and was greeted at the front door by the children. He was carrying a large cardboard box which contained a fresh turkey, Christmas pudding and mince pies, a tub of fresh cream, wine and chocolates and presents for all. He had insisted on making a contribution in return for the kind invitation. This was always his way of showing his affection for people he cared about......well, not always a turkey and maybe not a Christmas pudding, or mince pies, or a tub of fresh cream come to that, but it was always his way of saying something!...........Merry Christmas maybe?

The house was in total silence and the curtains were still drawn as the children ushered him into the lounge. They were staring at all the goodies in his box and pointing to the pile of presents at the bottom of the tree. 'We will open them when mum and dad come down.' they said excitedly.

'When will that be?' asked David.

'Not sure,' said Ben, 'they're still asleep at the moment, in separate rooms. Oh! and they're not speaking to each other.......anyway, Merry Christmas uncle Dave, would you like a cup of tea?'

As David reached the top of the stairs, I was just coming out of the bedroom wearing my dressing gown and slippers. I had heard voices downstairs and figured that the only other person my children would have invited into the front room at 9.30 Christmas morning would be Father Christmas himself.

As we sat in the kitchen drinking tea, I explained what had happened the night before. Same old story! I was supposed to be home by a certain time so that she could go off with her mates, to a Christmas Eve party at a night club.

Well it so happened that there was a bit of a party going on in 'The Phillippa' and I eventually rolled indoors at 11pm, one hour later than arranged. Her mates had gone without her so she had to follow on in a taxi on her own. It cost me £20! My suggestion, that we could have a cosy evening together over a bottle of wine and some nibbles, was met with a barrage of abuse. We certainly didn't have enough Vaseline in the house to assist the wine bottle on its suggested journey.

She wouldn't kiss me goodbye, so having first checked to see if the street door was still on its hinges! I settled down in front of the telly and fell asleep. I was still there at 4.30 am when she got home.

She rejected my efforts to make amends and would not pull my Christmas cracker under any circumstances. More Vaseline required !

She went upstairs and barricaded the bedroom door. I slept in the spare bed in Ben's room.

By the time I'd finished my story, David had prepared the turkey and put it in the oven. He was now making tea and toast for me and the kids. Ben took a coffee upstairs to awaken her majesty and wish her a merry Christmas. He explained that uncle David had arrived and that everyone was waiting to open their presents.

She arrived in the lounge a few minutes later and we got ready to hand out the presents. I looked across the room and said, 'merry Christmas, darling!' It was quiet for three seconds before Ben said, 'mum, dad said merry Christmas.' She looked at Ben and said, 'tell him to get stuffed!'

I looked at Ben and said, 'tell mum that David has used all the stuffing in the turkey.'

She looked surprised, 'what bleeding turkey? We haven't got a turkey!'

David smiled, 'Yes you have, I've bought you one for Christmas! Along with pudding and pies, wine and chocolates etcetera, so can we please think of the children and call a truce over Christmas. You can sort it out in the new year.'

Well surprisingly, she agreed! So we put some music on and opened our presents. David got on with peeling potatoes and sprouts whilst we all showered and got dressed.

He had always been a good cook and was quite happy to do the whole dinner whilst we enjoyed a family fun period in the lounge. He explained later that he needed to be doing something to take his mind off things. Although putting on a brave face, he was heartbroken at the thought of his own children and despised the bitch who had almost destroyed him.

We had already enjoyed two bottles of wine before the dinner went onto the table. By the time we had finished eating, it had become three bottles. Bloody good stuff it was as well!

Having pulled our crackers and put our party hats on, we were half sozzled by the time we settled down to watch a Christmas film......and were all fast asleep within half an hour.

David woke us up with a cup of tea at five o'clock. The room was cosy and we all had smug smiles on our faces. Christmas was going much better than I had imagined it would twenty four hours earlier! Later that evening, when the children had gone to bed, David played us the secret tapes which had been recorded over a two week period. He described the look on his wife's face on the Saturday morning that he showed them to her and let her listen to a couple of samples of her treachery. He had filled up two hour long tapes and still has them today but on CDs. I only hope that he hasn't mixed them in with his party music. Imagine that lot coming on.

Sadly, it was to be our last Christmas together as a family.

Early in the new year, Yvette and I decided to call it a day with the marriage. It was never going to work. We wanted different things out of life, which meant we would always be travelling in opposite directions.

I eventually found and rented 'Grace Cottage' in Ramsgate. Luckily, the children were old enough to understand what was going on, but it was still a very sad, tear filled day when I moved out.

Another chapter in my life that I could have well done without.

Another lesson learned, not only about life, but about myself.

I did love Yvette, but I just couldn't be the person she wanted me to be. It would have meant betraying myself and turning my back on the events which seemed to be shaping my destiny.

I was getting a lot of satisfaction from the various causes that I was involved in. I was making headway in several directions at the same time. It had become all consuming. In my mind's eye I had an 'in' tray labelled, 'Ambition' and an 'out' tray labelled, 'Achievement'.

Unfortunately, in the midst of it all, was a little flag with the word 'Selfish' being waved at me. I was being reminded that there had been a lot of 'selfishness' on my part. I will not insult your intelligence by pretending that I wasn't aware of this fact, but until now I had been able to justify this aspect of my behaviour by convincing myself that because there wasn't enough hours in a day, it was the only way to get the job done!

Various people voiced their concerns over my drinking but I had the perfect answer.

'It's not my fault that people keep wanting to buy me drinks, is it? To refuse, would be unsociable.'

That's the reason I drink - to be sociable. Mind you, since when has walking in a straight line been considered unsociable? I guess there are some things in life that you just want to believe.'

Chapter twelve: Partners galore.

1987 was the year for re-assessing my life.

So many things were happening and it was becoming almost impossible to keep up with all my commitments, something had to give! I realised that my biggest tie down was the shop. I was living at Ramsgate, working at Dumpton Park and Folkestone whilst running around sorting out the seafood business. Drumming up potential new customers, plus doing private functions and keeping in touch with fund raising projects - the one thing that I could now do without was my daily shop duties!

As much as I loved the racing game and all its wonderful characters, I could no longer manage the time or commitment needed to ensure a first class service to my customers.

After much soul searching and consideration, I realised that I could not walk away from the doors that were being opened for me. Nothing in my life could ever compete with the happiness and satisfaction I felt through my fund raising exploits. It was the thing I did best and the thing I enjoyed most.

I had a meeting with Alan Milton and he agreed to take over the whole betting shop business, lock stock and barrel. He would take over all financial and legal liabilities, staff commitments, the lot! This released so much time for me to do other things, it was like a breath of fresh air. I suddenly found myself with so much space to move around in, it was almost agoraphobic!

During the Spring of '89, we were hoping for a long hot summer, so as to pack the stands at Dumpton with holiday makers. The dog racing was always very popular, as indeed was the nightclub. At 10 pm, as racing finished, the club would open. Couples without children could let their hair down, have a few drinks and dance till midnight. Visitors who had attended the race meeting, were give free entry to the club.

In response to a phone call one afternoon, we were to receive a coach load of visitors, the likes of which we could not have envisaged in a million years.

The call had come from the production team of Only Fools And Horses and they were asking to rent the Car park for three days whilst making a Christmas special entitled, 'The Jolly Boy's Outing'. Obviously we said 'of course!', so for the next three days, I was to play host and chaperone to Del Boy, Rodney and uncle Albert.

They joined me for a meal in the restaurant on the first evening and we were joined by Casandra, Rodney's wife in the series. They were fantastic company and had me in stitches with their stories and behind the scene revelations. I could not help being impressed with how posh Buster Merryfield spoke. It transpired that he had been a bank manager for many years and had taken up serious acting after he had retired. The next day they were filming the market scenes. The car park had been transformed into an East End market. During a break in filming, I was able to get my children into some pictures that they'd kindly let me have taken. There was one of me and David Jason standing side by side. As the button was about to be pressed I muttered out of the side of my mouth, 'say something, Del'. He gave me that beautiful Del boy look and said, 'you plonker' We had a drink and Nicholas Lyndhurst sat Chantelle on his lap. Whilst pointing at me he asked her some funny questions about her dad.

The next day, we drove down to the car park at Walpole Bay, near Cliftonville. When we arrived, the cameras and lighting were already set up and there were several scenes being shot of the cast getting on and off the coach in various combinations. As they stopped for a tea break, a fire engine turned up. I leaned over the barriers and said to David Jason. 'What's happening now?' He smiled and said, just wait and see.......you'll like this bit!' This was the scene where they set the coach alight!

I loved working at Dumpton, always something going on. The fund raising events were becoming very popular and people crowded in to be part of them. Races were always well sponsored and the Stadium management were chuffed at the good publicity given in the Kent press.

On one memorable occasion, we had a 1940's night in memory of the Royal Marines Retired Veterans Association. Some had seen action at Arnhem and had lost friends and colleagues there.

Indeed my father always used to say to me, 'if you meet a man who was at Arnhem, buy him a drink'.

They needed two thousand pounds to buy a new 'standard' in commemoration of their battle achievements. We raised the money to purchase the flag which was subsequently blessed by the Bishop of Dover. It now flies with pride at every ceremonial occasion involving the Royal Marines.

Many of the management and staff at Dumpton Park had a close relationship with the Royal Marine Bandsmen based at Deal Barracks. They had been going to their concerts and Christmas pantomimes for many years. So when, on the 22nd of September 1989, the IRA bombed the barracks at Deal, killing 11 and injuring 22 bandsmen, the good folk at Dumpton wanted to help in any way possible.

I went on Radio Kent and announced an appeal for families and friends of the victims of this despicable atrocity which had shocked our great nation. I had just one week to co-ordinate the fund raising night at the stadium. I appealed to all who had ever helped us in the past to heed the call to action.

The response was incredible! All the races were instantly sponsored and we received an avalanche of raffle prizes to give out on the night.

The tickets sold out in double quick time and we were packed out on the night. People's generosity was overwhelming. I had originally set my sights on hopefully raising three thousand pounds. When the last guest went home and the counting was finished, we had raised ten thousand pounds! Not at all bad for one weeks organising was it?

I went on Radio Kent again to say thank you to everyone who had rallied to the call. I found the whole thing very moving and it served to confirm in my mind, something that we have always known in our hearts. As a nation, we will never bow down to tyranny.......on the contrary!

During 1989 I contacted Pontins Holiday Camps and asked if we could set up a sea food deal with them. They said that they would make a few enquiries and consider it. They probably did a survey on whelks and winkles and fed it into a computer. Low and behold, they got back to me and said that having looked at our portfolio and considering our location, we could set up shop at their Camber Sands camp down in Sussex. Their financial requirements were very reasonable, so I drove down to Camber and met the site management.

The camp was huge and I was excited at having gained a foothold with the big boys. I was given the use of a lock up preparation unit with refrigeration facilities and immediately introduced myself to the local sea food suppliers along that part of the coast. I also made contact with the Health and Hygiene dept and received a clean bill of health for our facilities. We commenced our services at the beginning of the 1990 season. It was good to be expanding the sea food business into holiday camps, and for a while it looked as if this was where the future lay. 'This time next year Rodney!'

I was now feeling a bit left out of things, being stuck down in Ramsgate. The Folkestone tunnel workers camp was now closed down, so that particular avenue to happiness was now just a memory. Some of the lads had moved up to Scotland to carry out a project and asked if I would be following on. I laughed and told them I had to draw the line somewhere. Anyway, the likelihood of finding a Scottish manager who would share the directors' drinks cabinet contents with me was probably rarer than rocking horse poo.'

In Spring 1990 I gave up Grace Cottage and moved in with 'Arry and his partner, Kim, at Sheerness. 'Arry and I worked well together and I wanted to be hands on with the Pontins deal. We had purchased a three and a half ton refrigerated lorry which doubled up as a preparation unit. We travelled to Billingsgate together every week, leaving at four in the morning and arriving back home in time for breakfast.

During the day, we would prepare food for the camp outlets. At Pontins we were required to work 7pm till midnight 7 days a week. We had employed two extra seafood sellers to go round the various activity areas on the camp whilst 'Arry and I ran the club and ballroom stalls. Tony was becoming more involved in the seafood selling and we had it in mind to train him up as a manager for our next Pontins camp! Also, we were still doing the camps on the Isle of Sheppey, Friday, Saturday and Sunday. We had five sellers going round them lunchtime and evenings. So we were constantly having to supply them with fresh food.

As the season wore on, we became busier and busier and were often still serving at one in the morning. The drive home after a hard day was becoming a daunting prospect. The management at Camber were very pleased with our service and were talking about giving us additional camps the following year. This was starting to look like serious business and my mind raced ahead to the following year. I was mentally preparing a recruiting scheme and thinking about buying another refrigerated van, setting up bigger stalls and getting staff uniforms etc.

In August that year, we had our one and only complaint from a customer. A lady told me that she'd had tummy ache the evening before and thought that it might be something she had eaten. There was no other complaint of that nature and I told her that it must have been something she had eaten elsewhere. She lived in Walthamstow East London, about a five minute walk from where my brother David lived at the time. How spooky was that?

The woman's name was Jackie and it transpired that she had an allergy towards the vinegar we were using. I know that to be true because I moved in with her in November of that year and married her two years later! Will I ever learn? Like I was so heartbroken and cut up over the other circus of horrors!

You may wonder what on earth I had to compare it with and how could I possibly make this next comment? But it was true....... **I missed family life!**

Jackie had a 5 year old son and a 3 year old daughter by her ex husband and was bringing them up on her own. She was able to be at home with them all day at present, but was wanting to start at teacher training college when the youngest had started school.

Now, with hindsight, I wished David had been there to talk some sense into me, with his home spun philosophy and pearls of wisdom!

Jackie and I spent as much time as possible together while she and her family were at Camber and after she went home from her holidays, we were phoning each other all night every night and getting very little sleep. I was slipping away to see her at weekends and was getting as big a welcome from the children as I was from her. I was getting on for forty years old and beginning to flag a bit at the never ending driving and moving around. Maybe it was the right time to start putting down some roots. Life had been fun at John's house but it was quite crowded at times and it was impossible to be alone with your thoughts. It seemed a good time to be moving on.

As Christmas approached, I got a phone call from the Pontins management asking if I would be able to take on a further two camps the following year. They were both in Norfolk, one was Hemsby and the other was Seacroft.

I had a meeting with John McCloud and put my cards on the table.

I was enjoying my new found family life and wanted to work around it in a manner which would be acceptable to my new partner. I had heard through a friend that William Hill were looking for experienced managers and were paying good money for the right people. I had applied for an interview to manage a shop in the north or east London area and would be speaking to them later that week.

I told John that I wanted to stay involved with the seafood business which I had started and built up. I would be prepared to reduce my share of the profits if John would take control of the workforce and run the business with me as a consultant. Jackie was a trained accountant and would do all the bookkeeping.

I would be prepared to carry out all negotiations and continue to help the business grow. Obviously, if it grew to a really serious size, I would reassess my commitment accordingly. The immediate requirement was to find somebody trustworthy to take my place in the field.

John said that he knew just the man. A divorced guy who had been working in seafood for many years and drank in a pub that he sometimes used. Apparently, the man had voiced an interest to buy into our seafood business a few weeks earlier. John said that he seemed to be a genuine guy and was prepared to take on responsibilities and put the hours in.

I subsequently met the man who was in his thirties and agreed with John that he seemed a nice genuine lad. He told us his name was Mark and that he was divorced and had no family ties. He convinced us that he was able to give a twenty four seven hands on commitment. It was like manna from heaven and he seemed perfect for the job.

We subsequently drew up an agreement and sold him 33% of the business for five thousand pounds. I retained 25% and John, who had the hardest job and biggest responsibility, would retain the lion's share of 42%.

It was agreed that John would take over my role and be responsible for the Billingsgate arrangement and the complete running of Camber Sands. The new partner would run the two Norfolk camps which were quite close to each other. He would be responsible for staff recruitment and paying Pontins their 15% of the total turnover for Hemsby and Seacroft each week. This had been our arrangement with Pontins from day one. Also, he would pay the seafood supplier cash on delivery. The seafood would be a mixture of fresh caught local delivery with specialised products transported from Billingsgate. This would arrive ready chilled for preparing on site in a preparation unit which had been made available at the Hemsby camp.

On reflection, I suppose I should have got to know the guy a bit better and driven up to Norfolk a bit more in the early stages. He certainly had the gift of the gab and was obviously a very confident type. Also, he had invested £5,000 in his future and assured us that he was happy with the arrangement and that he was confident he could handle everything in his stride. And so he should! It had all been handed to him on a plate.

I was pleased to find that an old colleague of mine from the Mecca days, a guy called Joe Kenny, was now in charge of William Hill recruitment. My track record was still on the computer and area manager, Lou Sutton, welcomed me aboard. It was January 1991. I had it in the back of my mind that if things didn't work out, I would drop back into the seafood business and carry on trying to build it up even bigger. As it was, I quickly settled down into the betting shop industry again and liked the potential of my shop which was in Mare Street Hackney, London E8.

I was now in David's part of the world and was seeing more of him. He was busy, what with his building company becoming established and taking on bigger jobs. One of his customers had a chain of dry cleaning shops, one of which was only a few doors away from my shop.

I had settled into family life quite nicely and was bonding well with Jackie's children. I had managed to convince her that lager was not the devil's brew and she quickly developed a taste for Stella Artois. Mmm, slightly chilled.....stirred not shaken......very nice miss Moneypenny!

The law in those days stipulated that betting shops had to be closed by 6.30 pm, although there was talk of extending opening hours in the summer. Parking was impossible near the shop, so I would travel to work and back each day on a routemaster bus. I had introduced myself to mine host at the pub opposite the shop and would have a pint before coming home each evening.....it gave the traffic a chance to die down a bit....rush hour and all that!

Easter soon arrived and the wheels started turning at the sea food depot ('Arry's front driveway). Easter was a week long season in those days, so the first opportunity for the new lad to show what he could do. He had been popping up to Hemsby to get himself familiar with the camp and staff and to organise a small unit that the management had agreed to let him use as a preparation unit. He had also lined up a couple of assistants at each of the two camps and fitted them out with the standard uniforms of white top and bottom with a yellow bow tie.

Mark was also helping out on the island, with the weekend pub trade and seemed very confident in what he was doing.

Finally, the summer season arrived and 'Arry' was having the pleasure of seeing a few old faces from the previous year. Camber was a great camp and many families would book the same weeks year after year. You could always spot them! They were the ones with three tables pushed together and a dozen people sitting around them. Always down the front, near the stage and dance floor. It was like a large family reunion.

Mark was up and running in Norfolk and everything appeared to be going fine. I say appeared because he was not the best person at keeping in touch. But when we spoke to him, he always said that everything was fine and going according to plan. We had to assume that he was talking about 'our plan'.

Meanwhile, back at the shop, I had a problem!

A group of black youngsters were smoking drugs and stinking the place out. They were also walking around with wads of money and placing large bets. I realised they were money laundering. I had also witnessed drug dealing in my shop!

I gave them a verbal warning and received a lot of foul language and threats for my trouble. I called the police and was told that it was a big problem in the area, they also asked me what I expected them to do about it? I was a bit taken aback by their attitude and told them I expected them to come and sort it out. They turned up and took the lads outside. One was arrested because he was carrying a large amount of drugs and money. He was also a known dealer. The others were warned about their behaviour earlier in the shop and officially told that they were all barred.

I related the incident to Jackie when I got home and used it to get the message regarding the dangers of drug abuse across to her children. Sadly, Jackie had to fill me in on how different things were in London compared to life on the Isle of Sheppey. Yes there were incidents on the island that were reported in the local paper, but we were never aware of gangs going around terrorising people and having no regard or respect for law and order. As my dear late father would say, 'Churchill would have spun in his grave!'

It was 3 am when the phone rang! It was the police at Hackney. 'You had better get down here quick, your shop is on fire!' Welcome to London!

William Hill took the opportunity to modernise the shop and all its facilities. I had been told by some of the older customers that the shop had been a nice place to meet and have a bet years ago. But since these kids had taken over the area, it had gone downhill fast and people would not come out for fear of being intimidated. The spineless gang that had challenged the law, never showed their faces again.

I created a good atmosphere in the shop, I even made the early birds a cup of tea and found time to have a chat about the old days. Some of them had fought in the war and many had lost friends and relatives whilst defending this country's values.

Word soon got round and all the old timers came back. They were amazed at the improvements to the shop and to the atmosphere in it. We stood together and made a pledge that never again would we let bullies or scumbags rule the roost. This was our betting shop and they would abide by our rules or else. Within six months I had doubled the turnover and received a 'well done' from the powers that be.

Chapter thirteen: Gutted!

A commendation from William Hill in June made me feel good, but I soon felt sick again when I received a kick in the proverbials from Pontins in July!

I had just returned, with Jackie and the children, from our first holiday as a family. A fortnight in Malaga on Spain's beautiful Costa del Sol.

We arrived home early evening clutching a hot bag of fish and chips, courtesy of our favourite fish 'n chip shop in Forest Road, Walthamstow. It's almost opposite the William Morris Gallery in Lloyds Park. So if you are reading this Tommy and Ann, that's a fish n chip supper you owe me for the plug!

We walked through the hallway towards the kitchen and I noticed that the answerphone was flashing with seven messages. As Jackie put the kettle on and started to set the table for our eagerly anticipated evening meal, I pressed the replay button. When I sat down at the dinner table ten minutes later, my appetite had completely gone.

Five of the calls had been for me. In the order that they were received they were as follows.

The first three were from our Norfolk seafood supplier. Anxious because he'd had no payment for his last five deliveries to Hemsby and Seacroft. And angry because Mark was fobbing him off with. 'Wait till Barry gets back from holiday.'

Message four was from Pontins' head office to say that they had not received any payments from our seafood operations at Hemsby and Seacroft and that our manager up there had not put out any food for three consecutive nights.

The final message was from John McCloud, to say that in response to a complaint from Pontins about the way the Hemsby and Seacroft business was being managed, he had driven all the way up there after shutting shop at Camber Sands. He arrived in the early hours of the morning and slept in the lorry until the staff arrived to open up the office. He discovered that Mark had done a runner with all the takings nearly £11,000. (£30,000 at today's prices). He had lied about banking his takings and had not paid the seafood suppliers or Pontins.

I felt sick as I phoned John McCloud at Camber Sands and asked him the most obvious question. Why did it take so long for these people to tell us what was going on?

It transpired that after the first query from the camp and the seafood suppliers, which was after one week's missed payment, Mark had bought himself time by saying that Barry and his family had gone on holiday to Australia for four weeks and that Barry had told him to say that he would settle up when he got home from his holiday.

Apparently, the seafood supplier was owed eighteen hundred pounds and was worried sick. It's understandable when you consider that it would be in the region of five thousand pounds by today's prices, enough to put a small business out of action.

Pontins on the other hand, were fuming, to think that I would take such a liberty without discussing it with them beforehand. Although angry, they had only realised that something was seriously wrong when the guy disappeared completely.

Because he'd become a full partner in the business, we had opened a subsidiary account at a local bank for Mark to pay money into whilst working in Norfolk. The arrangement was that after paying Pontins, the seafood supplier, his staff and himself each week, he was to bank the rest. He had been telling John the figures over the phone, including how much he was 'apparently' paying into the bank. The amount that he was banking seemed about right so John assumed that everything was OK. Unfortunately, he wasn't aware that Mark was putting the Pontins' and suppliers' money into his pocket instead of paying their bills.

John was paying **his** commitments each week and banking the balance into the main account which was only accessible by me and him. Being down on the south coast, he was getting his own seafood from Billingsgate plus local produce, so didn't know about the seafood supplier not being paid in Norfolk. Mark had held Pontins at bay with the Australia story. When he realised that I was due back from Spain, he knew it was time to scarper. Thank God he didn't have access to the main account.

I told John that our first concern should be the seafood supplier. He was a one man band who had purchased the food in good faith on our behalf. Apart from the moral aspect we would need his continued service....that's if we could get out of this mess.

The next day, Sunday, I drove to the supplier's house and put eighteen hundred pounds in his hand and apologised. He nearly cried with relief and said that it would have ruined him if he hadn't got it back. He also confirmed that Mark had told him I was away on holiday but had suspected that he wasn't telling the truth when he said he didn't have the money to pay him.

I phoned Pontins head office on Monday morning to apologise and try to repair the damage. The guy I spoke to, blamed me for everything, and said we owed them best part of two grand. Well to cut a long story short, he would not listen to my side of the story, which was genuine. The argument got so heated that I was on the verge of telling the guy to stick it where the sun don't shine, but he beat me to it and confirmed what I had feared from the moment he came on the phone. 'Pack your stuff and get off the camps, the contract is cancelled!', he shouted. I put the phone down and sat there gutted! All that hard work down the drain thanks to one stupid, greedy bastard.

I phoned John and broke the news to him. I felt terrible because I knew how hard he had worked to build up the business. He drove down to Camber and cleared our stuff out of the storage unit. He broke the news to his staff and supplier and drove back to Sheppey. He made a phone call and started back at his old taxi firm that night. The following week, he sold the refrigerated lorry, so we got some of our money back.

Over the years, I have often wondered how things would have turned out if I had taken on the running of Hemsby and Seacroft. If I hadn't met Jackie at Camber Sands I wouldn't have felt the need to play the 'family man' scene again! I doubt if there is an adult on the planet that hasn't looked back at some stage in their life and thought, 'what if, and if only?'

It's confession time!

There is a footnote to this story, the words of which I can hardly force myself to write, but it is total truth and nothing I can do or say will ever change that fact! Jackie hated Mark from the first moment she met him. She thought that he was a greasy, squirmy, lying bastard and didn't trust him at all. She warned John and me time after time, not to have anything to do with him. 'He's a wrong'un,' she would say. 'He'll have you over!' she would say....... OMG.....what if?

Jackie and I had a good talk about the future. She was a level headed person most of the time and always saw a situation from the right perspective. I had made a great start with William Hill. They told me that I had worked a minor miracle in the Mare Street shop and assured me that I would have a good future with them if I kept up the good work.

As mentioned earlier, there was a lot to be said for working regular hours and I wasn't getting any younger. I was beginning to get a bit tired of galloping about all over the country and the seafood venture going tits up had really taught me a few lessons about life. I might have been a crappy husband over the years but I had always been on the ball when it came to business. My trouble was expecting people to have the same attitude towards work as myself. Naively, I believed that giving someone a chance would bring the best out of them. I had got used to the hard work and loyalty input from John McCloud and unfortunately thought that this was how all people behaved, given the same opportunity.

With so much going on during the past year, my fund raising had been put on hold for quite a while. Jackie had been accepted for teacher training and had commenced a home study course. To my utter amazement I discovered that this would often require her to be sitting in front of the TV at 6am or sometimes as late as midnight, to watch some recommended lecture or training programme on Open University. One evening she made me a promise. If I settled down to a career with William Hill, she would help me with my fund raising exploits. I had been looking for an excuse to open a bottle of Chardonnay. God moves in mysterious ways. I poured two glasses and said, 'I'll drink to that!'

Mare Street was running smoothly and there were now so many 'good guys' using the shop, that if a 'baddie' wandered in, he would do a double take and walk out again. Some of my early bird regulars had their own tea mug behind the counter. One cheeky old timer even gave me some of his favourite tea bags to use and told me that his favourite biscuits were chocolate digestives.

Halfway through 1992, William Hill asked me to take over another local shop that was struggling. It was in Barnabus Road, Hackney Wick. I always thought Hackney Wick was cockney rhyming slang for prick. I didn't know it was a real place. Glad I didn't live there!

On my first morning at Barnabus Road, I walked in to meet the outgoing manager and to be shown the alarm system etc. He knew I was taking over but he didn't know which shop or area I had just moved from. He made me a coffee and we got chatting. He was one of the old school and had been with the company for over twenty years. Whilst talking about the changing times and how different things were these days, he said, 'this used to be a busy little shop at one time, but half of my old regulars now walk round to Mare Street. It's all been done up nice since they had a fire a little while back and the manager round there makes them tea and coffee and gives them a biscuit.'

I stifled a grin and said, 'what's it coming to these days....sounds more like a cafe if you ask me.'

'It's all changed,' said the old boy. 'They reckon there's gonna be night racing and gambling machines soon. Betting shops? Cuh! They're more like bloody holiday camps these days!'

My arse twitched as I stood up, 'I bloodywell hope not,' I said as I started to put the racing pages up on the wall.

My assistant turned up and after a few formalities the old chap held out his hand to shake. Good luck, Barry I'll pop in and see you if I'm in the area any time.'

Before I could stop myself I replied, 'It'll be nice to see you.....I'll make you a cup of coffee and get the biscuits out.'

He laughed as he walked towards the door. 'Well from what I've been hearing that seems to be the answer these days, mate!'

The shop was a lot quieter, a bigger challenge than Mare Street had been.

Chapter fourteen: Seymour sees the light

I was sitting alone, scribbling a few notes early one Friday morning, when I heard the shop door open. I didn't look up straight away until I heard a young voice say, 'ol fuckin 'ell, no!'

I raised my head and saw one of the young lads that I'd had barred from the other shop. He was standing there with a look of disbelief on his face. Well, up until that point, I had grown up in a world of giants, but this one was about my size. He must have been all of sixteen years old and probably weighed around nine stone. I tried hard not to smile as I said to him, 'come over here you.'

His face changed to a frown. 'Why, I aint dun nuffing man, what you want me for?'

I smiled and held my hand out. 'My name's Barry, we have a lot in common. I'm the new manager by the way, not the enemy!'

He walked over and shook my hand. 'I'm Seymour and it wasn't me that set fire to your shop......I told them I didn't want to be involved in all that and they said I was chicken. I made sure I was indoors wiv me mum when they dunnit.'

I laughed. 'How old are you?' I enquired.

Before he could stop himself, 'streetwise' kicked in and he said, 'I'm eighteen, so it's alright for me to come in here, innit?'

I nodded and smiled again. 'No problem at all, as long as you don't smoke pot!'

He laughed, 'that don't bother me....I don't even like the stuff, I don't even smoke cigarettes.'

'Neither do I, but I like a cup of coffee, do you know how to work a kettle?' I joked.

He started to relax, 'yeah, I make a cup of tea for my mum sometimes.'

'That's nice, what about your dad....do you make him one as well?'

'No, it's just me, my older brother and my mum. I never knew my dad, he done a runner when I was a baby!'

I kept a straight face and looked at him. 'Well that's a bit unfair, blimey you're not that ugly!'

He gave me a confused look and started to say, 'Ol no, I don't fink it was because I was......' He looked up and saw me laughing. 'Ol, you're 'aving me on'.....he started laughing. 'I couldn't believe it when you said that!'

I walked round the counter and opened the door to a small larder type cupboard. 'Well there's the kettle and the coffee and stuff but we need a pint of milk.'

He shrugged his shoulders and said in a matter of fact way. 'Yeah, well there's a shop round the corner, I'll go and get some if you like.'

I took a fiver out of my pocket and gave it to him. 'You can get some biscuits as well......if you like.'

He looked at the fiver and then at me, then he quickly shoved it in his pocket and almost ran out of the door. I figured that was the last I would see of him or my fiver, but five minutes later he walked into the shop carrying a bottle of milk and a large packet of McVities digestives.

He put them on the counter along with the four and a half quid change. He was smiling from ear to ear. 'I bet you thought I wouldn't come back...didn't ya?'

I looked at him and slowly shook my head as I lied, 'no, the thought never crossed my mind.'

We sat and drank our coffee and ate some biscuits. 'So how long have you been left school?' I asked.

'Nearly six weeks, I'm getting bored, it was more fun being at school.'

'Well it must have been exciting, doing your A levels and deciding which university you wanted to attend.'

He looked at me and laughed out loud. 'What you talking about? I never done no A levels ....I didn't even do O levels.'

'Well I can't understand this, what was you doing still at school when you was eighteen then?'

He realised what he had said and held his hands up. 'I aint eighteen Barry.......I'm only sixteen.....I'm not supposed to be in here really, am I?'

I was beginning to realise that here was a genuine victim of the system. He wasn't a bad lad at all. I nodded my head and smiled. 'Well as it happens, you are allowed to be in here. You're just not allowed to have a bet, that's all!'

He relaxed. 'I haven't got money for gambling.....I haven't got money for anything really. I've been trying to find a job, but nobody wants to train me. You've got to be able to do the job straight away, otherwise they don't wanna know.'

I felt sorry for him......he was a good lad living in a bad area. As I stood up, to my amazement he picked up the two coffee mugs and walked towards the toilets with them. I went back behind the counter and started to catch up on my paperwork.

When he came out, he had washed and wiped the mugs. He then walked over and put them back in the cupboard. Well I must be going soft because suddenly, I felt a wave of emotion roll over me and found myself saying. 'If you would like to give the windows and floor a wipe over you can put that four and a half quid in your pocket.'

'I saw the mop and bucket out in the toilet, is the floor cleaner out there as well?' he asked. I told him that it was, along with a pile of clean rags. 'Just give it a damp wipe and dry it straight away.'

The strange thing that occurred to me later that day was that if I had made that suggestion to him as he walked through the door earlier, I would probably have been advised to stick the mop and bucket up my bum, but he didn't flinch.

I looked up at the clock and realised that I would have a trickle of punters coming in soon to put their afternoon bets on, so couldn't risk them walking on a wet floor. He soon finished the floor and got stuck into both sides of the shop windows.

As he put the gear away I said well done and gave him his money. 'Promise me you won't spend it on anything stupid,' I almost pleaded with him, as he tucked it in his pocket. There followed a bit of uncomfortable silence, then he held his hand out to shake. 'Thanks Barry, you're alright you are.'

I'd had an idea whilst watching him work, so I left him with something to think about over the weekend.

'If you're not doing anything on Monday morning, pop in and see me around nine o'clock. We'll have another coffee and a chat and I might have some good news for you.'

As he walked away he turned and smiled. He patted his pocket and said, 'my first wages!'

I don't believe any kids are born bad. They just need a bit of love and encouragement now and then. These days we hear parents saying that they are working so hard to make ends meet, they just can't find the time to sit and talk to their children. I will agree it is an enigma, but you have to make time.

I've always believed in making the kids feel part of a team. Even if you know what to do within a certain situation, pretend you don't. Openly discuss the various options and carefully disguise your suggestions. Then wait for them to say the one you want to hear. Say 'that's a great idea' and give them the praise for being the one to suggest it. They get a great boost later by saying, 'that was my idea'. So simple, yet it works every time. As Del boy would say, 'that's yer psychology Rodney, knowing how the brain works and that!'

I made a phone call to a mate who owed me a really big favour and he agreed with my idea.   I

149

was totally chuffed. I couldn't wait for Monday morning.

I myself was having to exercise a bit of love and understanding these days, on account of Jackie's teacher training course having taken over her life and the house. The dining room table and floor were constantly covered with piles of papers of all colours and sizes. Some with labels on top or stacked in a certain order for quick access. The room was now a total no go area and we were eating our meals off trays whilst watching TV.

Over the weekend I told Jackie about my experience with Seymour and she was full of praise for the way I'd handled it. In fact, later that evening I saw her writing it down in précis form and I'm convinced to this day that she used it as part of her project on the psychology of teaching.

Monday morning came and I arrived at the shop dead on nine o'clock. Guess who was waiting on the doorstep? No it wasn't William Hill himself, he died in 1971. It was my child prodigy, Seymour.

He said good morning as I opened the door to the shop, then he walked over to the cupboard and took out the kettle. Having filled and put the kettle on, he took a pint of fresh milk out of a carrier bag. I remember looking at it and hoping that he'd bought it and not nicked it out of his mum's fridge. He made us both a mug of coffee and we sat down to have our little chat.

I was warming to this lad by the minute and I was pleased that my instinct about him had been right. All the cockiness had gone out of him and he had become a typical youngster starting out in life. I sat there knowing that what I had to tell him could change his life for the better......if he wanted it to.

'I need to ask you a couple of questions Seymour, just to make sure that I'm not wasting both of our times. I could have some good news for you.'

He nodded, 'that's alright Barry, ask me anything you want.'

'Do you take drugs and have you got a police record.'

'No! Nothing like that. My mum would kill me if I started all that sort of thing. She made me promise never to get in any bovver.'

'Why did you come into the betting shop last Friday?'

'I was just passing by and popped in to see the old boy. He used to be our neighbour years ago and sometimes he would give me a couple of bob to run an errand for him. That's why I was surprised to see you sitting there.'

'Yes! I heard your sudden surprise. What are you like on heights?'

'I'm okay....no problem, why do you ask?'

'I've had a chat with a mate of mine. A guy called Tony who runs a roofing company in Stratford. He's got quite a few lads working for him and takes on contracts all over Southern England. He said that he would take you on and train you to be a professional roofer. You would be expected to be punctual and work hard. Starting with sweeping floors and loading tiles and assisting the tradesmen. How quickly you make it to tradesman level will depend on you. Tradesmen earn between three to four hundred pounds a week plus overtime. Sometimes you may be required to work away from home for a few days in which case he will pay for your bed and breakfast. He will start you on one hundred pounds a week plus time and a half for Saturdays and double time for Sundays. How does that sound?'

Seymour sat there with his mouth wide open. 'One hundred pounds a week?'

He was shuffling around in his chair, which I believe was due to a mixture of nervousness and excitement. 'But why do you want to do this for me Barry, I mean those lads I was with gave you a hard time.......set your shop on fire and stuff!'

I laughed and realised that he had every reason to be surprised. I told him that I had done a few silly things when I was his age. But I was lucky enough to have a father who understood and he was there for me when I needed him. He let me find out for myself, just how hard it was to get a break and then he sat me down to discuss where we should go from there.

'You never had a dad to be there for you, so you found yourself in a wilderness. You're not a bad lad, Seymour, you just got into the wrong company, that's all. Like me, you found out the hard way. It's never too late to change your ways! Just choose your friends carefully.'

152

I finished off my 'job interviewing' by adding, 'your mates did me a favour when they fired the shop. It had to be completely refurbished and I ended up with the best little shop for miles around. It's like a social club round there now.'

He laughed, 'well let me know if you want this place done up and I'll give the lads a call. It's the least I can do after what you've done for me.....innit?'

I laughed, 'It's very kind of you to offer Seymour, but if every time I tell William Hill the place needs modernising and a week later it goes up in flames, they're soon going to put two and two together.'

He nodded and gave a wry smile. 'My mum goes to church on a Sunday and has been trying to get me to go. She says that all the answers to life can be found there and that I would never feel lonely. That's how I came to be tagging along with that bunch of losers......mum was at work all day and I was bored and lonely. I wanted to do something with my life but I didn't know where to start or who to speak to.'

'God moves in mysterious ways mate, maybe you was meant to walk through that door last week, maybe he didn't want you to feel lonely any longer.' I was beginning to sound like a preacher but I figured that what the lad needed in his life at this moment was an injection of faith. Maybe we all need that, every now and then.

He sat there nodding. 'So where do we go from here .....what do I have to do?'

I picked up the phone. 'Before I ring him up and introduce you, I want you to make me a promise. I want you to promise me, as a friend, that you will never tell lies or steal or bring shame on your family. Look after your mum, she is the best friend you will ever have. Work hard and keep your head down.'

He walked over and shook my hand. 'It's a deal, I won't let you down, Barry!'

As I dialled the number, I looked up at him and smiled. 'You'd better not, or I'll come round and set fire to your house.'

He started work the very next day and turned out to be a good worker and a fast learner.

The following Saturday, around 9.15 am, there was a knock on the shop door and I opened it to find a very attractive lady in her late thirties standing there. 'I am Seymour's mother, may I come in and speak with you?'

I put the kettle on and we had a good chat. She thanked me for helping her son and told me that his father had run off with a much younger woman when the child was three months old. She had been very concerned about the company he had been keeping and was so glad that I'd had a talk with him. She told me that Seymour had been getting up at 6.30 every morning and getting to work on time. He had come home the night before, and proudly put his first wage packet on the table. Then he said. 'I want you to have that, mum, and save it up so that we can buy our own house one day. He said he was sorry if he'd caused me unhappiness and promised that he would be a good son from now on. Thanks to you, my son has become a man.'

I appreciated her comments. That's all it takes to make life worthwhile in my book!

Saturday is a busy day and it was around four o'clock when Seymour came in and shook my hand. 'Thanks Barry, it's all worked out well. I've just finished and he's paying me up till five o'clock. He's a nice bloke that Tony and he said he was pleased with my work and my attitude. He told me that if I keep it up, I could be on the tools within two years.'

I had to carry on serving and settling bets as he talked but I managed to say, 'well done, congratulations. I met your mum earlier this morning and she is really proud of you, keep it up.'

He looked a bit embarrassed to think that his mum had come into the shop but he pulled something out of his pocket and said, 'I'm not old enough to take you in the pub and buy you a drink, but I would like you to have a drink on me.' He passed me a small bottle of brandy with a label attached. It read: 'To my good friend Barry. Thank you. From Seymour.'

I watched through misted eyes, as he turned and walked out of the shop. Putting something back into life is a good feeling.

Chapter fifteen: Francome & Coombs

On Monday morning there was a call from William Hill's head office asking me to attend a meeting there. They had an idea that they wanted to run past me.

As I sat on the tube, my mind and imagination was running riot. Was the New York branch not coming up to expectations?

I hadn't had a drink for over an hour and was experiencing withdrawal symptoms.

I walked into the office and sat down with a couple of the top brass.

The guy immediately facing me, picked up a sheet of paper and started to read aloud. 'Aha! Coombs.......Barry.... 'Before he could say another word I interrupted him. 'Erm...excuse me sir, but you've got that the wrong way round......it should read Barry Coombs!

He looked at me over the top of his glasses and slowly placed the sheet of paper back on his desk.

'Well, Barry Coombs.....we have a job that you may be interested in. We would like you to team up with John Francome and some others, to open all our new shops south of Cambridge and East of Oxford. We understand that you have a way with the public, so we would like you to warm them up for half an hour, introduce the celebrity and spend time giving out some freebies and answering questions. The celebrity will chat to them and sign a few autographs.   We are probably talking about one shop opening per month. You would receive your normal wages plus lunch and travelling expenses.

If they had asked me how I felt about spending a day with the seven times English Champion jumps jockey, I would have done it for nothing. As it transpired, John Francome MBE was a smashing guy and we became good friends. He had retired from riding in 1985 having ridden 1,138 winners, making him the third most successful jumps jockey of all time. In 1986 he was awarded the MBE for services to racing. After trying his hand at training, he became a television presenter for Channel 4 Racing and continued appearing until 2012. Also, in 1986, he started writing fictional novels revolving around the world of horse racing. He has written a book every year for almost thirty years, the first four being with James MacGregor. Over the years, John's books have been highly acclaimed with many featuring in the best sellers list.

In June 1992 I did a shop opening in Stamford Hill. I found myself warming up for both John Francome and John McCririck. Although feeling nervous to begin with, I soon got into my stride. Apart from the opening being a great success, I was to discover that John McCririck, although eccentric, is extremely knowledgeable about the industry. However, he does not appear to be over in love with bookmakers.

On 7th August 1992 Jackie gave birth to our son, George. Today, he is a plumber and works all over London with his company. (More genetics says David).

I worked hard at Barnabus Road and had it ticking over just right. I even put up a bit of tinsel and a few balloons to create a seasonal atmosphere for Christmas, which was just a couple of weeks away. A time for giving. I had attracted quite a few new customers and was getting occasional visits from some of my regulars round in Mare Street. My giving started before Christmas day though!

On the 16th December 1992 I had visitors of a different kind. Two scumbags walked in waving guns and, whilst holding a customer hostage, I had to 'give' them the contents of the tills. This was my first experience of looking down a gun barrel.

Jackie was appalled at how easy it had been for them to rob the shop and said that it must have been terrifying. Funnily enough, it was all over so quickly that I didn't have time to be frightened. It was later that night, when I thought about how it could have ended up, that's when it hit me.

William Hill were pleased at my developing track record of rebuilding shops that had fallen below turnover expectancy. As a result, at the beginning of 1994, they asked me to take over a shop in Turnpike Lane. They were of the opinion that I had the magic touch and knew the secret formula to building up a shop's profits. If they had glanced at my petty cash receipts for tea, coffee and biscuits.....there was a clue. Mind you, they wouldn't have seen the number of hours I'd spent cultivating new clients and making them feel a bit special when they walked in. Making them feel like one of the family, so to speak.

On the 8th April 1994 I was interviewed in my shop, live on GMTV. Fame at Last.

The other good news was that I had the fund raising wagon on the roll again. It was as though I had never been away.

As mentioned earlier, the seafood game was a lot of fun but it was so demanding of my time. I really missed being able to do the fund raising during that period, it was totally forbidden to even consider such activities at the holiday camps. Shame really because I would have had them travelling home in their underwear!

I was with John Francome doing our fifth shop opening together, when over a cup of coffee I happened to mention Channel 4s great racing programme Morning Line which was on every Saturday. John was a regular on the programme and I told him that in my opinion betting shops didn't have enough say in the way the racing industry was developing. The last memorable event, which had occurred back in 1986, was when TV screens were introduced into the shops and customers were allowed to watch live racing.

Let's face it, if it wasn't for betting shops, there wouldn't be an industry. Only a small proportion of racing fans go to the meetings!

John nodded in agreement and said that he would have a word with someone, maybe try to get me on the show to put my ideas forward.

Having realised what I had done I mumbled, 'Yeah! I suppose so, I mean I've got a couple of ideas, but what else would I talk about?'

He shrugged his shoulders and said, 'well,...... William Hill betting shops and the sort of stuff you and I talk about when we're together I suppose!

I smiled, 'I can't go on a Saturday morning racing programme and sit there for two hours talking about crumpet!' He laughed and punched me on the shoulder.

A couple of weeks later, I received an invitation to appear on TV. When I phoned to mention it to William Hill top brass, they already knew. The Chief Executive of William Hill in those days was John Brown. He was my hero at the time, having started as a board man and worked his way up to the top.

It was Royal Ascot time and John Brown asked me to meet him in his private box there. He wanted to know why I'd asked to go on Morning Line. Well, by the time I'd finished he was mesmerised. He poured me a glass of champagne and said, 'that's fine by me Barry, go get'em!'

And so it came to pass, that on Saturday 18th of June 1994 Barry the Bookie turned up on the popular racing programme, Morning Line. I was awestruck to be sitting next to and chatting to the likes of Lord Oaksey, John McCririck and seven times champion jumps jockey, John Francome MBE. I was so nervous, they had to drag me out of the hospitality room. They wanted me to be hospitable but not incoherent!

Whilst at Royal Ascot, I was asked to go to the press office and meet John McCririck who subsequently went through a few questions that he was likely to ask me on the day. I had written a few answers and anecdotes on a piece of paper.

On the morning in question, McCririck introduced me and without any reference to items discussed earlier, he set out to bamboozle me! His first question was, 'Barry! Where's all the fun gone?'

I looked across at John Francome...then down at my piece of paper and my first word on live television was...'Pardon?'

McCririck, as calm as a cucumber carried on, 'Well, I think, what the viewers are wondering is, where has all the fun gone from the betting shops?

This wasn't on the script and I didn't have a clue what he was on about, so whilst wondering if the hospitality room was still open, I mumbled, 'are they? Well!....... I think it's still there John.

John Francome could see exactly what was happening and jumped in to rescue me. He looked at me and winked and said, 'never mind about that, tell us about your first armed robbery.' Ironic isn't it, to think that talking about two guys threatening to shoot me two years earlier could ever become a comfort zone? But it was that morning. Thanks to John Francome, I was able to get comfortable for a few minutes and relax, before going on to other betting shop issues that had been agreed earlier. I don't get nervous that often but McCririck had me squirming that day.

The rest of the interview wasn't too bad actually, but as I travelled home, I was very aware of how difficult and nerve racking it must be for commentators on live TV to get it 100% right. They must be walking on eggshells sometimes!

I ended up opening around thirty five shops with John Francome and I always enjoyed his company. He was one of the kindest and most generous people I've ever met and we had some great times together. We were like Saint and Geavesie and never stopped laughing. One of the funniest and most heart warming moments I recall concerning John, happened early one Christmas morning. In fact, it wasn't really that early, it just seemed that way.

Jackie and I, having enjoyed a few Christmas Eve drinks and carefully putting the children's presents in their appropriate locations, had eventually gone to bed around 2.30 am. At 9.30 am the telephone rang! Jackie reached out and picked it up without even opening her eyes. I could hear someone merrily chirping away and Jackie was saying ....what?.....who?.....yeah, hang on. As she passed me the phone I whispered, 'who is it?' She pushed the phone into my hand and said, 'I dunno!......some happy geezer!'

It was John Francome full of the joys of spring, wishing us a very happy Christmas. We chatted away and I felt obliged to explain that my wife, 'isn't a morning person'. I did feel really embarrassed though. (On reflection, she was a right miserable sod in the morning!)

Later that day I was having a drink with David and I told him what had happened. He nearly peed himself and made me laugh when he said, 'for fuck's sake, the champion jockey of England rings to wish you a Merry Christmas and the politest thing she could say was, 'it's some happy geezer!'

It's amazing isn't it when sometimes in life, an innocent act of kindness and sensibility can have a catastrophic reaction. Don't worry I'm not referring to John's Christmas phone call. I'm referring to an incident that occurred late spring, early summer that year.

As mentioned, I now lived five minutes around the corner to David, in Walthamstow. As we had coffee together one Saturday morning I just happened to mention that I had the following week off to decorate a bedroom. I told him to pop in for a cuppa if he was passing by. By the way, I should mention that Jackie was a teacher in the school directly opposite our house. I should also mention that Jackie was not over enthusiastic about me having a drink during the daytime.

By Wednesday lunchtime I had painted the ceiling and woodwork and had started to paper the walls. The radio was on quite loudly and the windows were open. It was in fact a very hot day and paper hanging is thirsty work. I put the leash on our dog and walked out of the back door leaving it open and I left via the side entrance gate. I walked to the end of our road, turned left and walked past the convenience store and into

Lloyds Park recreation area. I strolled past the council workers who were doing a bit of landscaping and walked out the other side of the park and into the pub. One and a half hours later I returned home to find the windows shut, the back door locked and the radio turned off. There was a shopping bag on the kitchen table containing groceries that had been purchased at our convenience store. Jackie had obviously been home during her lunch break. I knew that she would have a moan at me for going down the pub, but this was part of my holidays for goodness sake!

I had heard the key go in the street door and was still hanging wallpaper when a voice behind me said, 'have a good drink at lunchtime did you?'

I looked round and there stood the UK champion wasp chewer with a face like a slapped arse. Whatever happened to, 'Oh that looks nice darling, hasn't it been hot today?'

I stepped down from my hop up and kneeled to trim the bottom of the paper. As I stood up again, I wiped my hands and said, 'thank you so much, darling. Welcome home, I'm so glad you like it. Yes it has been hot today and I really needed that quick pint!'

'Don't quick pint me, you were down the pub with David...enjoying yourself whilst I was at work!'

'What are you talking about? I haven't seen David!'

'You lying sod, his van was outside the park.'

164

'I don't know what you are talking about! Anyway, why do you have to come home checking on me? Closing the windows and doors and turning the radio off and snooping round! And you locked me out. Luckily I found the spare door key in the garden shed.

'I never touched the doors and windows and the radio wasn't even on.'

'Why are you such a liar? I saw the bag of shopping on the kitchen table so I knew you'd been home....you must have a problem! Snoop, snoop, snooping around.'

She turned and stormed off and I ended up cooking my own dinner. I was seriously concerned about her apparent control freak antics.

Saturday lunchtime I was upstairs sorting out some papers. Angela and William and George were in their bedrooms and Jackie was sat in the lounge playing games on her laptop. The back door opened and a pantomime voice shouted, 'hello boys and girls!' to which we all shouted back the time honoured reply, 'hello Mother Goose.' It was David.

As I walked into the kitchen and put the kettle on, his first words were, 'I've got a bone to pick with you. When I came by Wednesday lunchtime, your windows and doors were wide open and the radio was blaring out. These are dangerous times, bruv, you can't trust nobody these days. I turned the radio off and secured the place. Then I saw that the dog was missing and went looking for you over the park. I bumped into my fishing partner, Ken, who was doing some landscaping for the council. He said he'd seen you ten minutes earlier walking out the other gate with the dog. Straight away I knew where you'd gone so I turned round, got back into my van and went back to my job up in Leyton.'

As he finished speaking, the love of my life appeared in the doorway. I'm sure I detected a smile but wouldn't swear to it. As the kettle boiled I pointed at Jackie and said to David, 'we haven't spoken to each other for three days, thanks to you. We were both convinced that the other one was round the twist!'

We all laughed in the end and that episode became one of our favourite after dinner stories for years.

In the November I was asked to sort out a problem shop in Stamford Hill. There had been a lot of staff abuse and it was becoming difficult to get people to work there.

I had been there less than a week, when I found out why. A drunken Irishman vaulted over the counter and threatened to punch my lights out....because his horse had lost and he thought the race was fixed.

Whilst being backed up into a corner and holding a chair in front of me, I had already decided that, 'get out of my shop you arsehole' was not the appropriate comment at this stage. In my efforts to calm him down, I found myself explaining that although William Hill bookmakers were heavily committed to bringing horse racing to the forefront of public interest, we did not actually own or train any of the horses and that none of our staff ever rode them!

He calmed down somewhat and as he climbed back over the counter, he looked back and said, 'but do you accept that this sort of thing does go on......that they do fix these races sometimes.'

As I put the chair down and straightened my tie I agreed to accept that possibility, as long as he would accept that beating seven barrels of crap out of the betting shop manager was no guarantee that he would pick the next winner. (I was now buying time).

Three days later, whilst the shop was empty (we had only been open for ten minutes), I left my assistant in charge whilst popping next door for a pint of milk. I was gone no longer than three minutes and returned to find her arguing with a big Irish navvy! He was banging his fist on the counter and shouting abuse. I walked up to him and politely enquired, 'can I help you sir?'

He spun round and his eyes lit up as he grabbed me by the lapels. 'Aha! you're the bastard I want!', he growled triumphantly and banged me up against the wall. 'I want me fockin money! That dog last night should never have lost like that....I don't believe he was trying to win at all........he was drugged!' As I struggled to breathe, I heard a voice say, 'good morning!' It was the postman.

I was still pinned to the wall and could only squint my head to one side. Sensing that the cavalry had arrived, I grunted through my hand

167

restricted throat, 'I'm just explaining to this gentleman that we don't actually have any control over who wins the races. The postman put the mail on my counter and as he walked out he said, 'that's nice'.

As I tried desperately to prise open the hole digger's grip, I said, 'can we talk about this over coffee?'

He calmed down a bit and I was in the middle of explaining to him, why the race winner was 4/7 favourite, when thankfully his workmates walked in and took over. I was able to quickly retreat to the relative safety of the area behind the counter.

That evening, I got the Country Lover's Guide to Irish tours off the book shelf (as one does) and crammed my head full of interesting locations and the history thereof. I had never been to Ireland in my life, but by the time I went to bed I was an authority on the place.

I couldn't help feeling somewhat bewildered by the day's confrontation. As far as I had always been aware, Stamford Hill was a beautiful, peaceful, Jewish community. Among other claims to fame, it was home to some of the finest bakeries in the country and within a stone's throw of Tottenham Hotspurs football ground.

I was not aware that it was home to gangs of wandering, drunken, Irish turf speculators who had a vendetta against betting shop staff. It turned out that they came, courtesy of the various companies involved in the never ending road building projects in the area. Apparently, the local pubs had become battlegrounds at night due to so many of the road workers being in nearby B&Bs.

My initial problem was that the whole shop was Irish......all the Jews and Gentiles had been frightened off months ago. I had to get them back somehow!

My plan was simple. Get to know my customers personally, whilst they were sober, get the kettle on and learn about their families back home. Tell them I had been to Ireland several times and was planning to retire there. Pretend that my grandmother was Irish. Anything, to keep them off me and on the other side of the counter.

I put my plan into operation the following morning and by the time the first race kicked off at 1.30 pm I knew three Micks, four Paddies and a Sean. All it cost me was six tea bags two spoonfuls of coffee and half a packet of Digestives. Ah! begora, I was making headway alright.

I had the place running like a church social club inside of a year. The takings were up and the staff/customer relationship was really good. The best 'converts' could be heard calming their mates down and saying, 'don't go blaming Barry for that one now, it's not his fault you can't pick the winners. Just have some respect for his poor old lonely grandma, sat staring out of her window in..........where was it Barry?'

'Donegal!' I shouted!!

Chapter sixteen: Glass bottomed boat

In December 1995 I took over a shop in Grand Parade, Haringey. It came with built in menace and a first aid kit under the counter. Some of the customers had bits of their face missing and loads of scars. I immediately ruled out chicken pox and realised that I was living on Elm Street with a load of 'Freddies'.

There were several skirmishes and scary moments but I managed to get eight months service in before 2 pm on Sunday the 25th August 1996. A scumbag jumped over my shop counter wielding a knife and robbed the till. My female cashier was so terrified, she never came back to work. I was developing a twitch and ducking beneath the counter at the slightest signs of sudden movement. The sight of a hand plunging into a jacket pocket was enough to see me running out the back door and standing in the car park!

On March 24th 1997 I transferred to the 'Belvedere' in Lea Bridge Road Leyton E10. This was to be my absolute nightmare shop and made Grand Parade seem like a church picnic! It already had a terrifying reputation. On first opening the till I found a book entitled 'Tourniquets' How to stem the flow of blood.

I didn't have long to wait to find out why that was there. Welcome to Leyton!

On the 18th April, whilst on my way to bank takings. I was followed from the shop by three pieces of crap. I was attacked and robbed at knife point in my car as I sat at the traffic lights. The saddest aspect of this robbery was that people, sitting in cars around me, saw what was happening and just drove off. But the last laugh was on the scumbags. I had been carrying £2,000, but they escaped with just £35. Bloody amateurs! I was shaken up and sore after that encounter and was given a two week break to recover. Sadly, the mental scars take longer to repair.

On the 7th May that year, another historic event occurred. For the first time ever, betting shops were allowed to open on a Sunday. There were ten Sunday openings that year and it proved to be very popular. Within a year or so, the race courses had got their acts together and Sunday racing was a common occurrence. Betting shops were now open seven days a week.

I worked hard to improve the atmosphere in Belvedere and had bonded with most of the regulars by the time the next incident occurred.

On 29th August 1998, three muscle brains, strangers to the shop, started cutting up rough and were trying to get behind the counter. Before I knew it, some of my regular customers, had ganged up and had thrown them out into the street with a warning not to come back. I was totally chuffed at that show of support and bought them all a drink out of my own pocket.

On the 13th April 1999 another giant dog crap shoved a gun in my face and robbed the till. These were frightening times and my nerves were starting to play up. It was all very well becoming an expert at recognising different makes of guns and knives, but it was getting to the stage where, every time I heard the door open, I had to stop myself from diving on the floor screaming, 'don't shoot!'

On August 31st 1999, two ugly dog turds armed with knives, held me up and robbed me as I was walking to the post office to pay in some money.

I abandoned all hope of building up the shop turnover and making friends with the customers became secondary. Staying alive was the order of the day. It was me versus them!

What is it about April and August? Does the moon go into Psycho phase or something?

I was starting to defy the odds now and it was playing on my mind that maybe it was only a question of time before someone pulled the trigger or stabbed me.

You can understand now why I drink so much can't you? I drink to forget.......to forget the previous day!

I was given a month off to recuperate. I cancelled my membership to the 'Blockbuster' club and no longer watched gangster DVD's. It was tantamount to bringing my work home!

Quite rightly, the management were sharing my thoughts and feelings. They were becoming concerned about the effect that these hold ups might be having on me.

In February 2001, mercifully I was moved to Winchmore Hill. This was to become my favourite venue. It was quite simply a fantastic shop in a very respectable area, full of great customers. It was like a breath of fresh air.....God knows I'd earned it.

I quickly settled into life at Winchmore Hill to begin what I have since come to regard as my 'golden period'. This was also the year that saw the introduction of a new form of gambling in betting shops.

FOBT machines. or to give them their full name, Fixed Odds Betting Terminals, were introduced to a few shops to test popularity. To begin with, they were numbers machines. Similar format to the National Lottery. Within two years they were in all betting shops and had become very sophisticated! It was like having a mini casino on hand. Poker, Pontoon, Roulette, you name it, there was a machine somewhere that would accommodate you! FOBTs, were rapidly becoming the major attraction in some shops and were drawing in many new customers, they were also making shed loads of money!

By the beginning of my fourth year at Winchmore, I had stepped up the shop rating by two grades. This was not only good for William Hill and my ego, but also beneficial to my bank account. Apart from the excellent racing services on offer, I had upgraded my Sunday morning 'early birds' tea and biscuits to include roast potatoes, cheese and assorted nibbles. Some customers would actually be waiting for me as I opened up. It was like some sort of social club with a free breakfast thrown in. I was 'spanking' the two nearby betting shops and joy of joys, **my charity work was back in full swing.**

My wife, Jackie, was now involved in the fund raising and really had the bit between her teeth. She had come to realise the joys of helping underprivileged children and had even encouraged a few of her colleagues to help out. We ended up with a really enthusiastic squad and I take my hat off to all of them. After expenses, such as hire of films and projectionist and various bit of stationery etc, an average night would raise around five to six hundred pounds for the chosen cause. We were sometimes doing two a week.

On 20th February 2004, Jackie and I celebrated our ninth wedding anniversary. She had accepted and adjusted to my ever changing timetable which was supposed to be five days on, two days off. But, due to various 'festivals' and classics overlapping and the occasional staff shortages due to sickness or holidays, it was not unusual for me to do seven on three off or even nine on four off. It made no difference to me because on my days off, I was seeing people and organising fund raising events and loving every minute of it.

One of our most popular packages was 'Race Nights'. These were held at various clubs and pubs and schools around London and the home counties. I would hire a projectionist plus racing films, dogs or horses. The films were in sealed canisters and would be picked out one at a time by members of the audience. I would never know the results until the race finished. The betting would be carried out in Tote fashion so the punters would be creating the favourite by volume of bets and paid out in accordance. Always a good social event, creating a tremendous atmosphere and a few hundred quid for a deserving cause.

Most organisations that asked us to do fund raising events, already had their 'worthwhile cause' picked out. But we would always suggest worthwhile causes in the event that they just wanted to do something for the benefit of the community. On a couple of occasion I encountered tossers who wanted us to put on a fund raising night in their local pub so that they could put it in their pockets. But I always insisted on the full details, address, phone number etc. of the benefactors and checked them out before agreeing to act on their behalf.

March saw the welcome arrival of the Cheltenham Festival once again. Such a popular event and an absolute magnet for thousands of Irish punters, who would cause every hotel and B&B for miles to be packed to capacity.

A special treat was in store for me when William Hill asked if I would play host to newly retired top Irish jockey, Norman Williamson. For three days, I was to chaperone this legend and interview him from 9am until 10am each morning in the main William Hill office at Cheltenham, asking him for his opinion on each race and picking up a few tips along the way. All of this was being broadcast live on William Hill radio in every shop throughout the country. It went so well that we were also given a live ten minute slot on Channel 4's Morning Line on the final day. I was having thoughts of my own chat show one day.

An interesting footnote here is that on Friday 21st May 2004, Derek Thompson and I opened a new shop in Palmers Green. One year later I was to become the manager of that shop.

Meanwhile, back to 2004. The holiday season had arrived. Jackie always took charge of family holiday arrangements. We were off to Benidorm for the week to stay at the 'Solana' Hotel. Or to give it its real name, 'Sol Pelicanos'. As you are probably aware, this location went on to find fame and fortune in a very successful TV series, Benidorm. We actually stayed at the Sol Pelicanos four times in all. Whilst filming was going on, they put the name 'Solana' on the wall.

During a holiday in Cala Tarida on the island of Ibiza, we enquired about going for a trip on the glass bottomed boat, to watch the fish swimming around beneath us, whilst enjoying a sandwich and a cup of coffee. The receptionist at the hotel told us that all you had to do was to join the queue and sit down on the boat. Someone would come round for the money whilst you were travelling out to where the fish were.

We arrived at the jetty dead on 10am and saw that there were two boats with queues waiting to get on. We joined the shortest queue which was also for the largest boat. As we started to move forward onto the magnificent cruiser I said to Jackie, 'this one's probably a bit dearer but what the hell, we're on holiday.'

We sat down and looked around at the luxurious fittings and noticed that everyone was dressed in beautiful designer clothes. We were wearing T shirts, shorts and flip flops. As the boat cruised away from the jetty we were gazing out to sea. Suddenly, there was a polite cough and we turned to see a waiter holding a tray of drinks. 'Would you like Pimms or Champagne he enquired? We grabbed a glass of Pimms each before he had a chance to change his mind. We then noticed that there were other waiters walking around offering people a selection of delicious looking canapés. We were given a plate each and proceeded to fill them with salmon, prawn and pate canapés plus olives and grapes. As our waiter went to get lemonade for the children I looked at Jackie and muttered, 'bloody hell! this is the one to be on isn't it, how can they do all this for a fiver?'

As we sat there stuffing our faces and enjoying our second glass of Pimms, a glamorous lady in an immaculate two piece white suit sauntered over and said to Jackie, 'Oh, you've brought the children....how splendid.....well done darling!'

Before Jackie could answer, Angela tugged the lady's skirt and asked, 'what about the fish?' As the women attempted to wipe a pate coated hand print off the bottom of her white skirt, she looked at Angela and said, 'what fish, sweetheart?' Angela put her hands on her hips and impatiently replied, 'the fish we've come to look at through your bottom!' As the startled and bemused woman stood up sharply, I quickly added, 'she means through the bottom of your boat.'

The woman closed her eyes and nodded slowly. As she opened them again she said, 'would you excuse me for a moment, and walked away.' About two minutes later a man in uniform walked over and said in a broken accent, 'good morning, I hope that you are enjoying yourselves. May I ask whose guest you are today? As I looked at Jackie she was just taking a 50 peseta note out of her bag and was holding it up to the man. 'We're on our own, thank you and nobody has asked us for our money yet.' The guy smiled. 'Your little girl is wanting to see the fish but I am afraid you are on the wrong boat for that. This is a private party and these people are here as guests of one of our ambassadors. The glass bottomed boats are much smaller.' I started to apologise but he put his hand up. 'Please, there is no need for apologies. I can see that this is a genuine mistake. Unfortunately, we are three miles out to sea and do not return to Cala Tarida until four o'clock this afternoon. I have spoken to my boss and he is happy for you to remain as his guest until we reach San Antonio. From there you can get a bus back to Cala Tarida In the meantime, please enjoy a glass or two of wine and some canapés. You will have a good story to tell your friends when you return home.'

As the cruiser docked at San Antonio, we said thank you and farewell to our host and walked down the gangplank onto the quay. As the party revellers walked off into town, we became aware of another family, dressed as we were. They were standing and gazing around them in a bewildered state. I walked up to the guy and said, 'excuse me, could you tell us how to get to Cala Tarida?' He laughed and said, 'I was just going to ask you the same thing. We wanted to see the fish but got on the wrong boat old boy!'

It transpired that we were a one hour car drive away from Cala Tarida. After wandering around to find toilets and bottles of water, we stopped a taxi. The driver spoke very little English but we were able to understand the words eighty pounds! The earlier elation had worn off and we were now beginning to feel sorry for ourselves. Dragging three leg weary, irritated, glass bottomed boat yearning children around in thirty degrees of sunshine is not the most fun packed day imaginable. We were eventually guided to a bus stop and waited an hour before stepping onto a bus that could take us 'half way' to Tarida. Another half hour wait before stepping onto a bus that took us to Tarida town centre and finally a ten pound taxi ride from Tarida town centre to our hotel.

We had left the hotel at nine thirty that morning to go on a one hour boat trip to see some fish. It was now five thirty in the afternoon. We were collapsed on our beds, sunburned and knackered. The last sounds I heard before passing into oblivion were, 'Angela! If I hear the words glass bottomed sodding boat once more! I'm going to bury you here.'

On returning from Ibiza, we had a few days rest and were off again. This time to Las Vegas for a week. This was mum and dad's bit of indulgence but the kids loved it as well. We went to Vegas five times in all, and once treated ourselves to a helicopter ride to the bottom of the Grand canyon for a slap up Champagne lunch. Apparently, this venue is one of the hottest places on earth. I can vouch for that! You've no idea how much champagne and beer I had to consume in order to remain cool!

Vegas is everything you imagine it to be, but you have to be sensible. Pay all your bills in advance and ration yourself to as much spending money per night as you can afford! Leave the rest in your safe. Las Vegas is jam crammed full of temptations.

Chapter eighteen: The C word

Towards the end of August 2004 I was back into the swing of things. Not only was I working late nights at the shop, I had also fully committed myself to a variety of charity fund raising appeals when at home. Rest periods?.....never!

I had been feeling run down for a week or so and laid the blame on working long hours. I was feeling increasingly tired.....too tired and was falling asleep whenever I sat down. Also, I was losing weight. Although suspecting that this was more than just, 'feeling tired', I hoped that my suspicions were wrong and continued to work for another week.

On Monday 13th September I had a lay in and finally got out of bed at 10am. I felt really ill! It was my day off, the house was empty. As I put the kettle on I had a panic attack and realised I had to seek medical advice. I went to see my doctor who said that he would arrange for some blood tests to be carried out in the next couple of days. I was not happy with that. I was struggling to stay awake and feeling increasingly disorientated. Something was seriously wrong! I decided to take myself to hospital! How I drove my car to Whipps Cross I will never know, but the fact that I did, probably saved my life.

As is par for the course in London, the hospital waiting area was packed. I walked over to a 'serving hatch' sized opening and described my symptoms to the young receptionist who was sitting behind it. I didn't have a note from my doctor, which turned out to be a big mistake on my part. She hardly looked up as she said in an arrogant tone, 'go home and sleep!' She was a civilian, so what exactly qualified the stupid bitch to make a spot diagnosis and offer her 'remedy' is beyond me. I felt panicky again and emphasised my anxiety to the receptionist I really did need to see someone. With an air of superiority, the arrogant bitch replied, 'okay, but I'm putting you down as low priority, so you are in for a long wait!'

By this time I was feeling very unsteady and needed to sit down before I fell over. As I searched for an empty seat, I struggled to understand the belligerent attitude of the receptionist. It was also beyond the comprehension of the consultant who examined me at 4.30pm and arranged for my immediate admission. He was extremely annoyed at the attitude of the receptionist and said that he would definitely look into it. I like to think that these days the ex receptionist is doing a job more suited to her. One that doesn't involve making life and death decisions! Cleaning the toilets for example! Perfect place for a piece of shit like her!

You can speak to people who have known me for thirty years and they will tell you that I am very placid and easy to get on with. I apologise to anyone who is offended by my comments regarding the receptionist, but every time I think of that episode in my life, it fills me with sadness and anger. How dare she treat me like that! Please do not defend her attitude, she was an arsehole!

I had sat down in the waiting area at 12.30 pm. I felt absolutely terrible and knew deep inside that something was seriously wrong with me. But thanks to the arsehole in reception, I sat for four hours without food or drink, drifting in and out of sleep. I was finally woken up by a nurse at 4.30 pm. Doesn't it fill you with pride and gratitude to be living in one of the more 'civilised' countries??

The doctor examined me and ordered immediate blood test. The results were given to him twenty minutes later and suddenly I was a priority admittance. I was given oxygen, put on a drip and moved to a preparation room. By this time there were various people coming and going and I was drifting totally out of it at times They gave me a jab and struggled to insert a central line into my main artery via my upper chest.

After puffing and moaning the doctor said, 'sorry about this, it's a central line that we are trying to get in. I remember replying, 'I don't care if it's fucking Victoria line.....just get it in there!' That's the last thing I remember before waking up in a ward at 10.30 pm.

They had managed to stabilise me in time and proceeded to carry out several tests over the next couple of days, at the end of which they sent for Jackie and we were spoken to by the consultant surgeon. He informed us that I had a growth in my throat and they suspected that it might be a rare cancer. I was immediately being transferred to Barts Hospital in order for one of the country's leading authorities on this particular type of cancer to be able to carry out some tests and have a look at it himself. I prayed to God that I was going to be in the right hands.

How I didn't have a heart attack I'll never know. Being told that you have cancer is one thing, but learning that it is a very rare one! Trust me, I was on the verge of becoming almost unique. The last time I'd heard this kind of talk was back in my teens, when my father had looked at me appealingly and said, 'why can't you just be normal, Barry?'

Professor Monson was *the* man at Barts. He greeted me with the reassuring words, 'Barry, you're not to worry! You are not going to die......not for a long time.' I only hoped that his idea of a long time was the same as mine. Old aged pensions and the over eighties club sprung to my mind!

After more tests and another scan, the consultant broke the news to me and Jackie. I had 'parathyroid cancer'. It was one of the rarest cancers known; there had only been four previous cases at Bart's. If caught in time, it was one of the easier ones to treat. The parathyroid gland's purpose is to regulate the production of calcium.

He read the report and comments made when I'd been admitted to Whipps X, and told me that I'd had enough calcium in my body to kill a horse. Also, if I had followed the receptionist's advice, it was unlikely that I would have woken up again. I was already massively over the danger level when arriving at Whipps X. Apparently, I had defied gravity by driving to the hospital and walking into the waiting area that day and would certainly have died within 24 to 48 hours of a heart attack if I had left without being seen by a doctor. He told me that the panic in getting the central line into my main artery was real and getting me stabilised had become critical.

Because I had woken up in a ward, four hours later, I thought that they had put me out, but he told me that they had given me a local anaesthetic not a general one, I had simply passed out and slept. It had been a close call apparently, too bloody close for comfort. It is amazing how, even though we feel so ill, we put off going to the doctors, in the hope that it will go away.

I was operated on and sure enough the tumour had grown **inside** the parathyroid gland. That's why it had been so difficult to detect. It was just beginning to break through the walls of the gland. An eagle eyed junior doctor had spotted it and drawn it to the attention of his superiors. So glad they didn't show it to that receptionist!

There can't be many people that have had their throat cut and lived to tell the tale. As the days went by I was beginning to feel my old self. I was up and about and constantly looking in mirrors for signs of a scar. I was doing this on one occasion, when a patient from another ward was passing by. The colour was back in my cheeks and I was smiling because he had stopped to see what I was looking for. 'What's wrong with you then, you look a picture of health?' he said, as I turned to face him.

'Oh! It's nothing really,' I replied, 'I've just had my throat cut and I was looking to see if it's left any scars.'

The smile disappeared from his face. 'Fucking 'ell!, you're a cool one you are, what was it a gang fight or a mugging?' he muttered.

'Neither,' I laughed, 'I was just passing by and was bored, so I whipped out my knife and went......' There was an abrupt, 'stop it Barry, don't tell him that! It's nothing to laugh about!'

I had been overheard by a staff nurse and she was not amused. As she briskly walked away with a face like a slapped arse, I leaned over and whispered in the guy's ear, 'she did it! but I'm not allowed to tell anyone.' I turned and walked quickly back to my ward.

The next morning, the consultant gave me one last check up before I was allowed to go home. I casually asked him how they'd managed to stitch my throat without leaving any scars. He explained to me , that in some operations they are able to use super glue and this had been one of them. I still find it difficult to walk past a tube of Araldite without picking it up and kissing it.

Whilst in Barts, I found myself in the next bed to a remarkable gentleman. His name was Gordon Campbell OBE. He was quite a famous journalist actually and was often referred to as the 'Father of the Press Gallery' in the House of Commons. He'd had a leg amputated due to cancer. Sadly, the Big C does nobody any favours. Gordon was a great comfort to me during that emotional period and I found myself feeling more sorry for him than I did for myself.

Gordon and I became good friends and due to us being from totally different backgrounds we were fascinated by each other's journeys through life. He loved my stories about the betting shops and my family's trips to Las Vegas. Because I was the more mobile of us, I used to get him his newspaper, The Times, each morning and fetch his breakfast. I would also run him a bath. I used to put some of my Body Shop strawberry bubble bath in and he loved it.

Gordon used to tell me stories about famous people he'd encountered during his long and illustrious career as a top journalist, most of which was spent in the press galleries in the Houses of Parliament. After I was discharged, I kept in touch with Gordon and his family. He is without doubt the bravest and most awe inspiring person I have ever met and it was an absolute privilege to be his friend for a while.

I have an annual m.o.t at Barts to see if there are any further problems developing, but fingers crossed...so far so good. This year marks the tenth anniversary of that sad period in my life. I got lucky, but it still took the skills of a dedicated team of experts to get me through something which could so easily have had a different outcome. So sad to reflect on how unfair it is these days, that the actions of the odd 'nutter nurse or orderly' that has slipped through the vetting system with false papers, can make the headlines and subsequently get some of the dedicated, hard working staff of the NHS tarred with the same brush.

I, along with millions of others, also have strong feelings about people such as footballers and pop star divas **picking up** in one week, the same money that a trained nurse takes ten years to earn. I say picking up because they certainly don't **earn it.** As far as I am concerned, it only serves to hammer home what a truly despicable world we live in. A world gone mad!

Rooney, Ronaldo and Messi and so many others play entertaining football. Plus, I love to watch a good show and listen to the beautiful girls singing their heads off. Especially the ones that constantly run the risk of developing serious hyperthermia! Two or three grand each a week plus a few fringe benefits would give them a nice lifestyle. That is what most of us would agree to! But to earn fifty times more than a surgeon or the Prime Minister and five hundred times more than a nurse is absolutely scandalous and the sign of a sick society..... total lunacy! Sadly, we are all to blame, we should hang our heads in shame for standing by and allowing it to happen!

On Monday 15th November, after a period of convalescence, I went back to Winchmore Hill and was on light duties for a couple of weeks. It was good to be back, I had missed the daily grind like mad.

I began 2005 with a new lease of life and a couple of ideas on how to build up business even more! There was excitement in the industry due to the introduction of new space age technology. It came in the shape of an EPOS machine: Electronic Point Of Sale. This machine would acknowledge the investment, calculate the odds and settle a bet within seconds. No more marking up the results on a paper or settling every bet with a red pen! The standard procedure which had been in place for over a hundred years, was now obsolete.

One Monday in February, I visited Gordon Campbell in Guildford Hospital. I had kept in touch with him and had heard from his family that he was unwell again. I wanted to cheer him up and although I could see that he was laughing through the pain barrier we had a few laughs. He was so happy for me, having got better and 'beaten the swine!' He wished me and my family a happy and pain free future. I wish that I could have known him longer, he was a truly lovely man. Sadly, he passed away a few days later. God bless him.

Apart from the EPOS machine, there had been another new element come into my life. An area manager named Richard Poole. I had a meeting with him on Monday 11th April. He told me that I was being moved to a shop at Palmers Green. It had a reputation for being a manager's nightmare, with incidents of violence, mainly Eastern Europeans, smashing up the gambling machines. The fact that I was still recuperating from my serious illness cut no ice with Richard. Saying a sad farewell to my favourite shop full of lovely people at Winchmore Hill, was probably one of the saddest events in my life.

Chapter nineteen: Straws & Camels' backs

On Monday 18th April 2005 I started work at Palmers Green. Looking back I came to realise that I was beginning to hate Mondays. The shop did indeed turn out to be a manager's nightmare! A problem shop, with police in attendance on so many occasions, we were on first name terms. The previous manager had been badly beaten and robbed in the shop The irony here was that I had originally opened this shop with John Francome a year or so earlier. It was plagued with incidents of violence. Fights, arguments and staff abuse were common, due mainly to a high population of Eastern Europeans in the area and half of them being in my shop. I found it hard to understand why having come to this country to build a better future for their families, they were happy to gamble it away in betting shops.

Although I was able to improve the turnover somewhat, it was not possible for me to work my usual magic and improve the overall atmosphere in the shop because of the language barriers. They seemed to think it was 'us against them'.

I was therefore quite happy to be moved and in 2007 I was asked to take over a shop in Bowes Park. My sense of relief was short lived, as I discovered that this shop was as bad as the last. Eastern Europeans were constantly losing their tempers and taking it out on the machines. Any attempt to calm them down was met with a hail of abuse! Indeed, my efforts to calm one guy down were rewarded with a knife being waved in my face. He was removed by some of the regular customers and the police went after him.

In recent years, this state of affairs has gradually become more common in betting shops up and down the country and is now a serious problem. In the thirty four years that I have been in the betting industry, I have worked with all colours and creeds and have made many wonderful friends along the way. There is not a biased or racial bone in my body. I merely speak the truth and tell it like it is! Sadly, I am sorry to say that it is a whole new ball game out there now and until the laws are changed, incidents such as those described will continue to occur.

I reached the end of my tether at Bowes Park and was close to resigning when in May 2008 I was moved to a shop in Rupert Street, China Town. It was a busy shop which suited me just fine but I was finding the journey each day, very stressful. I was still in remission with my cancer and what with evening racing and the late journey home each night, my doctor was becoming concerned over my energy bank. It didn't help matters when in July of that year, another scumbag got behind the counter and robbed the till. My mental resistance barrier was also wearing thin.

In Sept 2008 I moved to what was to be my final venue. Situated among a parade of shops in Hatch Lane, Chingford. It was ten minutes from where I lived and had everything needed to survive, right on the doorstep! i.e. Fish n chip shop.

Bakers, Off Licence and a bloody great police station five minutes down the road. This was soon called into action!

On 31st Dec 2008, 9 am On New Year's Eve, two masked men armed with guns, ran into the shop and demanded I open the till. I was standing behind a floor to ceiling metal structure. I told them that the tills were locked. They grabbed a couple of chairs and started to smash down the metal and glass framework above the counter. I phoned the police and under a new system I just needed to say 'armed robbery' and my postal code, they were on their way immediately. I was trapped behind the counter and the robbers were just about to vault over the counter when we heard the sirens. The guys ran off and within minutes there was a helicopter circling above the shop with the armed ground police giving them instructions.

As I sat amongst the twisted metal that ten minutes earlier had been my shop counter, shaking so badly that there was more coffee on the floor than in my mug, the words to a song were ringing in my ears. 'There's got to be something better than this!' Happy New Year Barry.

I was at Hatch Lane for almost four years and although that was my last armed robbery, I'd had a few narrow escapes from punters wanting to punch my lights out because they'd lost their money.

The problems were mainly over the casino machines. Seeing their horses and dogs being beaten might have been a bit of a bummer but most of the punters were aware that we could not possibly have any effect on the way the animals had run. The casino machines, however, were a totally different kettle of fish and the punters had all sorts of weird and wonderful theories about them. One guy accused me of having a secret switch behind the counter. He said I could control the number of wins and how much the machine would pay out. Another guy had the notion that everything was controlled from head office, that they could see what was going on and make you lose when they wanted to. Another claimed to have worked it all out! He said, 'when the shop is shut, you take all the big wins for yourselves and just leave the small ones.' I felt like saying, 'yeah! small like your brain,' but he was kicking crap out of the machine at the time so I thought I'd let him burn up a bit of energy first. Where are we heading with this problem? Are we to see bouncers on the doors of betting shops?

In the end, the strain of not knowing what was going to kick off next started taking its toll on my nervous system. I was put on medication by my GP and asked by William Hill to attend a counselling course through the Employee Assistance Programme. After further meetings with the management, I was obliged on the 24th June 2011 to attend a Harley Street Occupational Health Clinic. I was interviewed at length by Dr Clare Piper the resident O.H. Physician. Her initial recommendation of a three month plus break from work and the associated stress, to be followed by a re-assessment examination, was honoured by William Hill.

Unfortunately, my recovery was greatly hampered by the steady deterioration of relationships at home. Jackie had been a senior teacher for a few years and was wrapped up in various events to do with her position.

The cancer period had taken its toll and we had been stretched to nearly breaking point at times. On the subject of cancer, I am pleased to report that I have been in remission for over ten years. I have cut back on my drinking and still have an annual check up at Barts.

The development of my 'nerves thing' was a gradual process. As you grow older, life doesn't bounce off so easily and the bruises take longer to heal. But I hadn't reached the stage where I was dressing up as Napoleon Bonaparte or collecting string. Not that there's anything wrong with that of course. (I have to be aware of any 'real' Napoleons and string collectors out there - political correctness and all that).

My wife had become impatient. Me being at home all the time. Watching TV......going down the pub at lunchtime......having a kip on the settee in the afternoon. Events, which you and I know are essential towards 'getting well soon and making a full recovery. How on earth could anyone be jealous of what I had been through in recent years?

If someone close to you had been ill, would you deny them a period of convalescence or the manner in which they managed it. Especially if it had been recommended by a Harley Street specialist? Of course you wouldn't. Okay, Dr Piper never said anything about going down the pub being an essential factor in my recovery programme........on the other hand, she never said, 'whatever you do, don't go down the pub!'

I'm laughing about it now because Jackie and I are divorced and I'm retired, but the last couple of years in our house was purgatory.

In all seriousness, William Hill tried very hard to accommodate me, with periods working in the public relations dept at head office. Mind you, a public relations officer who keeps jumping up on a chair doing chicken impersonations, is not conducive to the recruitment programme! (Not really). Plus, I was still doing shop openings with Tommo, which was always a good day out.

After great patience and understanding on both sides, it was eventually agreed that we had reached the end of the road and that it was time for me to be put out to graze....in pastures new as it turned out. I embarked on a series of events, dinner dates etc. to celebrate my career with William Hill and I left with their good wishes and a golden handshake

As mentioned earlier, I do not have a racist bone in my body. In recounting my experiences based on 33 years in the betting industry, I can only tell it like it is. Telling a punter who has had a few drinks and just lost £200.00, to get out of your shop, whilst he is smashing up a machine, is a very dangerous business and the outcome can be very unpredictable. I am sorry to say that by far the worst culprits for violent behaviour of this kind in recent years have been Eastern Europeans. Having said that, I would rapidly add that, over the years, I have enjoyed the company and conversations of a great number of really nice people from this part of the world. The vast majority of them are equally pissed off with the irresponsible behaviour of some of their fellow countrymen because it is getting them all a bad name. Life is hard enough for them as it is.

The laws and punishment for violent behaviour in a public place are laughable and certainly do not deter re-offenders. Even after being found guilty of several such offences, the likelihood of a custodial sentence is still quite remote.

Crimes of violence are on the rapid increase and the streets are no longer a safe place. Being on your own in an empty betting shop at ten o'clock at night is not the greatest comfort zone on earth. Sadly, incidents such as the ones referred to in my story, are happening in jewellers, Post Offices and shops all over the country every day of the week. We live in violent times. The police can no longer cope and only attend a few chosen incidents. The criminal fraternity just stick their fingers up and laugh at them. Prisons are bulging at the seams and prisoners are being released early to make way for new ones. Having said that, through their own insistence, betting offices now have a higher degree of security than most other shops and the police alert process is high tech.

William Hill is a great organisation to work for, in my opinion, the best. Always at the forefront of new innovations within the industry. Over the years they have set standards that competitors have struggled to match. They have an excellent staff relationship policy and have been very good to me. In particular, they were extremely supportive in my hour of need. The period when I had cancer put a severe strain on my family life, but I never had the worry of wondering if I still had a job to go back to. The company's attitude was, get well soon and come back whenever you are ready. For that, I am eternally grateful.

The betting industry gets bigger every year and offers a bright future for youngsters with the right attitude. I was given the chance to expand a few new ideas within the comfort and security of a long established and reliable system. William Hill still leads the way, winners by a mile.

Chapter twenty: Barry the Charity

I was given the label, 'Barry the Charity' by the Editor of the William Hill in house magazine. I was appearing in it quite regularly as a result of my various exploits and was often referred to as 'North London's favourite son! The magazine had been following my fund raising activities with growing interest over the years, and I was proud that William Hill was often at the forefront of my schemes to help those less fortunate.

As I walked into a meeting one day, to discuss our annual fund raising night at Walthamstow Greyhound Stadium, someone shouted 'here he comes, Barry the charity.' We all laughed as he added, 'Barry, when you walk into a room, there is an air of expectancy,' I smiled and said, how do you mean?' He replied, 'simple mate, because when you leave, we all expect to be a lot poorer!' There was loud laughter and as it died down, he added, 'look around you Barry......look at them all frantically hiding their possessions and nailing their wallets to the floor!' The place erupted.

The William Hill organisation was always very supportive of my charity campaigns. They knew that I regarded my charity work as 'something I was always meant to do'. It was not possible for me to forget the early days, when my emotions were constantly stirred by the incredible courage displayed by so many young children. Some, including my own sister, born with serious afflictions, others dying of incurable diseases. There were times when I struggled to understand how God could let this happen.

I would often stand and stare at a hospital children's ward and experience mixed emotions. One feeling was of satisfaction that I had been able to help in some small way to put a smile on a few faces. The other feelings however, were ones of guilt and regret because in the grand order of things, I was only one small, insignificant person and that although my efforts were appreciated, my contribution was a spot in the ocean compared to what was needed. How I wished at such times, that I could be rich and famous. I could mix with people who could easily afford to put something back into a world that had been so good to them....the lucky ones.

I can never thank enough, the many people who, over the years, have worked tirelessly alongside me. Those who shared my dreams and aspirations and gave me so much encouragement and support. You know who you are and I salute each and every one of you. We gave it our best shot didn't we, but we were always aware of the many who could, should, have joined in.

It's a strange but true observation on my part, that over the years, those who didn't have much, were the first to give. And those who had plenty, always managed to find a reason as to why they shouldn't part with any of it! Erm, just remind me! What was it that Jesus said about rich men and the kingdom of heaven?

As mentioned earlier, my initiation into fund raising came via my daughter, Chantelle, and her sick friend at school. Raising money to brighten up the life of Rosie Miller was exciting and gave me an insight to people's love and generosity at a time of need. Not only had I learned how to do fund raising, which left me with a sense of achievement, it also made me aware of that unique feeling one gets when doing something really worthwhile.

When Curly Wilson asked me to help him with the Margate Hospital project, I was surprised to find myself responding in a most positive manner. After all, £35,000.00 was a huge sum of money at modern day prices. It was like someone saying, 'I want you to take the hat round and help me raise £150,000.00' If it hadn't been for the Rosie Miller experience, I would have regarded Curly's request with trepidation. As it was, I felt confident that together we could achieve our target.

I have already described the feeling of elation at being able raise such a sum of money in a relatively short space of time. Nervousness was now nonexistent. I was brimming with confidence. The question now was not, 'could I raise the money', it was, 'how soon can I raise the money?'

After fulfilling the Margate Hospital dream, there was no stopping me. I was more convinced than ever that this was what I wanted to do. It was like a calling! Everywhere I looked, there seemed to be a deserving cause! I was determined to integrate the fund raising with my career.

I worked at Dumpton Park Greyhound Stadium, doing summer cover in charge of the restaurant and night club, plus promoting public relations. Over a period of three years, I carried out around twenty charity fund raising events at Dumpton Park and would fill the place with local celebrities and a few well known faces from TV and the theatre. It got to the stage where local businessmen would want to be seen to be involved in Barry Coombs' Charity events. Not only because their hearts were in the right place, but because they knew the newspapers would be there, plus a few of their local competitors. I can now reveal that Barry the Charity sometimes played naughty tricks on people! The trick was called, 'one against the other'. I'm sure that most of you will have already worked out what's coming.

On a hot summer's evening back in 1990 the function area and restaurant at Dumpton was packed with black ties and posh frocks. It seemed that champagne corks were popping every five minutes. Two of my guests on that occasion owned roofing companies, one in London and one in Kent. I will refer to them as Bill and Ben!

Bill, I knew quite well. He drove a Jaguar and had a big house in one of the top residential areas. Children at private school and all the trimmings of a wealthy man. He was well know in Kent for his generosity in supporting good causes.

I'd never met Ben until that night, but had heard that he drove an Aston Martin, had expensive taste in clothes and shoes, and owned a mansion set in three acres of land in a posh part of Hertfordshire.

I would normally run a raffle and do an auction of gifts donated by local companies for that purpose. A signed football shirt was always a competitive lot for example. The regulars knew that at some stage I would announce the sum raised on the evening and thank everyone for their support. It was also standard practice to say a special thankyou to a person or company for a sponsored race or a particularly large donation. This would often result in them taking a bow and receiving rousing applause.

I was talking to Ben, who didn't know Bill was a roofing contractor until he walked over and stuck a cheque for two hundred pounds in my hand. 'There you go Barry, another wonderful evening. It's always a pleasure to be invited and to help your suitable cause on the night.'

I shook his hand and said, 'Thankyou Bill, you have put a smile on so many sad faces over the years. The children will be so grateful. Your generosity is always appreciated mate.'

As Bill walked away, he smiled and said, 'my pleasure Barry, only too glad to help'.

At the risk of repeating myself, back in the late eighties, that was like someone sticking a grand in my hand today!

Ben looked down and saw that the cheque was for two hundred pounds. He also noticed that it was a company cheque....a roofing company. 'Seems a nice guy Barry, local company is it?'

The antenna raised from the top of my head and I could see the smiles on the children's faces getting wider and wider! 'Yes, he's a smashing guy Ben....always gives generously. I always take that as a sign that someone is doing very well for themselves, don't you?'

I acknowledged an imaginary wave from someone behind Ben and as I started to walk away. I could see that he was deep in thought.

Ten minutes later, as I stood holding an empty champagne glass, Bill's wife held up a Moet bottle and mouthed the words, 'would you like a glass of champagne?' I felt like shouting, 'is the Pope catholic?' as I walked over and kissed her on the cheek.

As we stood talking, about how the kids were getting on at school etc. a voice behind me said, 'sorry to interrupt, just thought I would give you this, Barry.' I turned to face Ben! He was waving a cheque for all to see and making a point of letting Bill see that it was **his** company's cheque......for five hundred pounds! 'I've made it out to you Barry, I hope that's okay!', said Ben as he held it up under my nose.

I nodded. 'No problem Ben, I can endorse it to be paid into the children's fund. That's a very generous gesture Ben, business must be good. (I know exactly what they want to hear). As he turned to walk away, he glanced at us and agreed, 'mustn't grumble Barry.....mustn't grumble mate.' Bill looked at me and laughed, 'he's obviously not putting two teenagers through private education ready for university. Mind you, I'd be chirpy if I was getting the prices he does up in London.'

The champagne was flowing like water and one hour later I was half p...p...p.... champagned!! The evening was going great and I was walking around with a fixed grin on my face. This was spotted by Bill, who walked over and said, 'you look very pleased with yourself....what's the joke?

I knew that Bill liked a laugh and I couldn't stop myself. He obviously realised that the cheque waving episode was all for his benefit and was totally nonplussed. I chuckled as I told him, 'I keep wanting to go over to Ben and say, 'Bill's just given me a cheque for another five hundred quid, making seven in all!'

Bill rolled up and said, 'do it Baz, I dare you to do it!'

I laughed at the thought of it and the possible repercussions, but decided against. I was grateful for Ben's donation, it was a lot of money and I didn't mind him putting on a show of the presentation. He received loud applause and a few handshakes when I announced it later.

The evening was a great success and we raised over five thousand pounds towards special equipment for a local hospital.

During my time in Ramsgate, I put on around twenty fund raising events at Dumpton Park, which together raised over one hundred thousand pounds. Also, due to my sea food activities at various pubs and clubs on Sheppey, I was often asked to help out with raising money for things such as primary school equipment, items for youth clubs etc. Also, I was advising friends in London to raise money for their children's schools. I was even getting letters of thanks from various NHS departments, for supplying 'essential equipment'. Pardon me for thinking this was the responsibility of the government! There were many more similar, small events over the years, but they added up to around fifty five thousand pounds and put smiles on hundreds of faces.

Changing the subject for a moment, a very strange thought has just entered my head. I worked at Dumpton Park Greyhound Stadium until they shut it down to build a housing estate. I organised seven annual dinner/dance fund raising events at Walthamstow Greyhound Stadium until they shut it down....to build a housing estate. Barry the Bookie.....kiss of death, or does he have an arrangement with Barretts the House builders?

Today, I work as betting manager/consultant at Towcester Park racecourse where I and several others have been instrumental in setting up a new Greyhound track there. My business partner Chris Page is the new racing manager at Towcester. He's the best in the business having managed the 'Stow' stadium for 26 years and offered his consultant advisory services to several others.

Ah! But wait a minute, what's this I hear? I have recently been informed that Towcester Park Estate (which is massive) has been granted planning permission to build several new executive houses! No pressure there then!

I told brother David about the planning permission during a chat about various things and he phoned me up a couple of days later. He said, 'I had a strange dream last night Baz! I dreamt that you were standing alongside the greyhound track, watching a race. Suddenly, a bulldozer turned up and a lorry containing two bricklayers and a cement mixer. As the mixer was unloaded, they walked over with their trowels in their hands and stood beside you. The dogs came hurtling around the bend and one of the bricklayers tapped you on the shoulder and said, 'ow long you gonna be mate?' I love my brother but he's a bastard at times!

Top man at Towcester is Chief Executive Officer, Kevin Ackerman. He is one of the nicest guys I've met and has been totally supportive during the two years spent setting up the new Greyhound track project. This is the first of its kind in England. At a time when dog racing stadiums have been closing down, Towcester had the bottle to 'take a gamble' and build one and the whole racing industry is watching to see how it prospers. The early signs are very encouraging, as people have come to realise that Towcester is a family orientated venue. We have some great ideas lined up to encourage family attendance in the future. I laughed a couple of weeks ago when I asked a young couple with a boy of about twelve years old how they were getting on? They were just walking into the restaurant for a meal. The man said to me, 'I backed the losers in the first two races and

Robert here said, 'let me choose them, dad!' I gave him the pen and he chose the two outsiders in the next race. They came first and second and I had the forecast five times. I picked up seventy eight pounds. The number six dog won the race and I asked Robert why he'd chosen it. He said, 'because it runs in a Newcastle shirt!'   It was his favourite football team.'

So what are you thinking at this moment in time? Barry Coombs is an acquired taste? In some people's eyes..... yes, I think I am! I've done my share of bowing and scraping over the years and have often conceded on issues that I have considered to be correct in my assessment. I have learned to be gracious in victory and humble in defeat. The second part not being difficult when the final comment from 'them upstairs' is, 'so that's it then, you definitely agree?'

It's a great feeling to be right about something and to watch the egg being wiped from the faces of the doubters. But when I have been proven wrong, my strategy has been simple. Watch with interest as the right approach unfolds, learn as much as possible and come to understand why that was the correct choice and most important of all remember how it works! Because next time round......with a new audience.....that idea will be mine! I shall be praised from the highest and acclaimed for my wisdom and labelled, he who can do no wrong.....The Chosen One.

Chapter twenty one Tommo & Francome

Meanwhile, getting back to my early career, it was now 1991, I was in my second year with William Hill and my second year with Jackie, (who was now pregnant) and the children. I was in the midst of organising a fund raising event to benefit children in St. Ann's Hospital in Hackney. During a visit, I noticed a ward full of elderly patients and popped in for a chat. I noticed that they didn't have a TV set in the ward and I asked them if they would like one. A rousing, 'yes' went up so I shouted, just leave it to uncle Barry and walked back down to the children's section. I contacted a guy I knew at Dixons of Wood Green, (not to be confused with Dixon of Dock Green) and he did me a blinding deal.

On the 7th August 1992 Jackie gave birth to our son, George. Eleven days later, on the 18th August we presented St. Ann's Hospital with a brand new TV for the old people's ward. A big thank you to Dixons, who helped me to make a lot of people happy.

On 16th December 1992 I was held up and robbed at gunpoint at my shop in Hackney Wick. Eight days later, on Christmas Eve, we took a big bunch of flowers and a present for each person to open, to the old folks ward at St Ann's. What a contrast of emotions that week was. Looking down a gun barrel one minute and a ward full of smiling faces the next! Two extremely opposite feelings. I know which one I preferred.

As we wished them a merry Christmas and said goodbye, they switched on their new TV set and settled down to watch a show. Christmas is a wonderful time of year, a time for love and forgiveness as we celebrate another very special event over two thousand years ago!

The 'Race Nights' mentioned earlier were proving very popular and we were doing two or three a week at one point. It was quick and easy to set up and we were able to tell the pub/club owners how to generate interest prior to the event in order to get more bums on seats and maximise funds for their chosen charity. On average, they were donating £600 to their charity for each event. Some were putting on regular events and we got to know their patrons quite well. It was a shame that we were driving and had to keep a clear head. If we'd accepted all the free drinks offered, we would have become full blown alcoholics. We were not too proud to accept the odd bottle of wine to take home for later though!

During the next few years it was to be the race nights that constituted the bulk of my fund raising activities with the odd local charity appeals thrown in. With a new baby in the house and Jackie having embarked on a teacher training post graduate course, I was expected to pull my weight. In all fairness, it was Jackie who was taking the calls and booking us in for race nights and she would accompany me on most of them. Baby sitters were close friends and family members and were much easier to come by in those days.

In June 1994 we went to Curly Wilson's daughter's wedding in Rochester. Curly and I hadn't met up for some time and it was great to see him again and catch up on all the stories. Jackie drove that day which is just as well because by the time we left for home, I couldn't even walk!

One week later it was my famous encounter with McCririck on Morning Line and I was wishing I wasn't sober! Once again a big thank you to John Francome who could see what McCririck was up to and stepped in double quick. John's a no nonsense guy with a wicked sense of humour. We became good pals and carried out 34 William Hill shop openings together. I knew he was on mega bucks and jokingly said to him one day.

'We work well together don't we?'

As he put his coffee cup down, he sat back in his chair, took a deep breath and spread his shoulders.

'We certainly do Barry....like Saint and Greavesie.'

'Or Morecombe and Wise,' I suggested!

He smiled. Yes, you're the one with the short fat hairy legs.'

I nodded and agreed. 'As long as we can make them punters laugh and want to come racing....it's a 50-50 thing really isn't it?'

He nodded and said, 'it certainly is Barry, teamwork, that's what it's all about...teamwork mate.'

I nodded and said, 'do you think we should split the money down the middle?'

He looked at me to see if I was serious, then his face cracked up as he laughed and said, 'Piss off!'

Today, John is a successful writer with 30 best sellers to his credit. We still do Christmas cards and I often smile as I look back with affection at some of our chats.

Another 'young man' who has become extremely inspirational in my career is Dereck Thompson, or Tommo as he likes to be known. He is without doubt the most thorough person I have ever met. A stickler for accuracy and attention to detail. As he walks alongside the winning horse, congratulating and interviewing the jockey. I would put money on the table and state that if the horse had one testicle larger than the other, Tommo would notice it. He is a total perfectionist and never misses a trick. He is also a master of facial expressions. If we spot something during our shop opening projects, he will look at me and pull a face. It speaks a hundred words and I just totally lose it. Richard Fox also has that effect on me.

Tommo is an absolute credit to his profession and a natural showman. Nobody does it better and if anyone should have their own chat show it is him.

Sadly, Tommo's chances of a knighthood disappeared the day he beat Prince Charles in a horse race. Granted, it was for charity, but Tommo could not help wondering about the wisdom of riding it out. Luckily, there were several people who, on the day in question told Tommo that the future King of England would not have appreciated being patronised. In the end Tommo agreed with them and enjoyed his moment of historical triumph. However....had it been Henry VIII!!

Like me, Tommo has had cancer. Mine had been eight years earlier and I believe that he was grateful to have someone on board who had gone through the agonising hours of wondering. He was a surgeon's nightmare. He actually requested to be fitted in after Royal Ascot was over! Thankfully, he was in the best possible hands and has been in remission for some time now.

Tommo is on the celebrity payroll at William Hill and over the years we have carried out 58 shop openings together. The public turn up to be given a selection of freebies and to ask a few questions about various aspects of racing coverage. Also, they like to hear a few snippets of behind the scenes gossip. I don't think I ever heard a question that Tommo couldn't answer.

It has also been my privilege to work with Richard Dunwoody, Richard Fox, Peter Scudamore, and Pat Eddery and my nemesis, John McCririck. A 'punters man' who sometimes views bookmakers as the 'enemy'. Admittedly he is very colourful and controversial, but in my opinion, John is an absolute must on any racing programme.

February 20th 1995 saw another milestone in my life. Following several hints from our children, Jackie and I decided to get married. We both liked the taste of wedding cake and it seemed a good idea at the time!

We booked a day off work and knocked up a few sandwiches, got some beers and wine in and made a few phone calls. It was a great 'do' with all the traditional trimmings of an East End wedding. We had a great knees up in the front room of our house. The budgie got out and escaped through the window and someone threw up in the front garden! Auntie Gladys had been on Bacardi and coke all day and went missing around 3pm. she was found an hour later, wedged between the garden shed and the greenhouse.

I have to admit that due to a build up of nerves, I'd had a few 'stiffeners' leading up to the ceremony, plus an immense amount of 'Stella' and champagne! I don't remember much after the knees up. It was David who later told me where he'd found aunt Gladys, an incident that she strenuously denies to this day. He's a daft bugger sometimes he really is!

Also, we sent photos showing the registry office wedding and the knees up, to Country Life Magazine, but they didn't get published It was probably a busy week for society events.

My brothers and I inherited our mother's wonderful sense of humour. She was the most incredible lady. East End born and bred and the youngest of fourteen children, she would do anything to make you laugh.

I remember the family gathering to celebrate her eightieth birthday. The house was packed and the sound of laughter was deafening. Mum had disappeared upstairs and after fifteen minutes or so we began to get a bit worried. Suddenly the door opened and in she walked dressed up as Old Mother Riley. It was an outfit that she had worn to win a fancy dress competition a couple of years earlier. We absolutely rolled up as she carried out her 'Arthur Lucan' routine. (He was the original Old Mother Riley). As she sat down, she said, 'this is what I want it to be like at my funeral....everybody laughing and being happy. David, who was sitting beside her, turned and said, 'don't worry mum, we won't let you down, I've already written a few jokes.'

Sadly, my mother had to cancel coming to my wedding due to ill health. She had been diagnosed with stomach cancer eighteen months earlier and was now taking heavy doses of morphine each day. She was a wonderfully brave lady and bright as a button right to the end. She passed away on 24th July 1995, aged 84.

Sad to note that both my weddings were marred by sadness. My father died suddenly on the 12th November 1976, one month before my first wedding on 11th Dec.

In all, I did over one hundred and fifty charity race nights in London and the home counties. On many occasions I would get to meet the recipient in whose honour the event had been organised. On a few occasions their gratitude would extend beyond a simple 'thank you' and a shake of the hand. As they expressed their feelings in a little speech, calling it a 'tug of the heartstrings' would be an understatement.

Race Nights were fun, but they often involved quite long journeys around London, through heavy traffic. After a hard day's work they could be quite daunting. I was missing the 'big occasions' being surrounded by people loaded with cash and looking for a purpose in life. Someone once said, 'money can't buy happiness' but I knew a lot of exceptions to that rule. I had seen the effect that people's kindness and generosity had on so many sick children. Money can buy happiness if it is spent wisely.

On the 3rd November 2001 I held a Gala Night in the Goodwood function hall at Walthamstow Stadium. The stadium owners, the Chandler family, had kindly given me free use of the premises for the fund raising party. They were totally supportive of my ambition to establish an annual event that local businessmen and their families would be proud to have on their social calendar. I had managed to obtain sponsors for all races on the big night and had a pile of gifts to raffle and auction. The crème de la crème was an Arsenal shirt signed by all the players and management, a gesture generated by a phone call request from yours truly. This was to be repeated by the Gunners every year for seven years, for which I am extremely grateful. Not a bad achievement considering I'm a Spurs supporter. The shirt became the highlight of every auction and was keenly contested.

The catering was great and everyone commented on the superb food. It was a black tie/

posh frock do and there was a good turnout of local businessmen and several celebrities. The entry ticket price just covered the catering and bar staff wages on the night. I didn't want to frighten people away with exorbitant prices on the first event, I just wanted to ensure that they would come and see the potential and then encourage their friends to come next year. It was early days as far as I was concerned. A sprat to catch a mackerel you might say......or in this case, a prawn cocktail to catch a salmon mouse.

Everyone had a great time and I was able to give £3,000 to Wish Upon A Star. This enabled terminally ill children to be sent on holiday to Disneyland in Florida. Back in 2001, that seemed a lot of money, but it was well worth the effort especially as things were to get even better as the years rolled on. By the way, Richard Branson donated a 'free jumbo jet flight' each year for this event!

Meanwhile, on the work front I was getting stuck in at Winchmore Hill. So much so, that in March 2002 my efforts won me the William Hill Employee of the Year award. Luvely jubbly, nice little bonus.

In May of that year I was able to send a group of youngsters and staff, from a local children's home, on a week's holiday at Butlins. They had the time of their lives and I received lots of photos and thank you cards. We had our picture taken to appear in the local Guardian Gazette. As the photographer sorted us out, one little girl turned

216

to me and said, 'I wish you was my dad'. If I had a mansion house and pots of money I would make sure they all had as normal a life as possible.

I managed to smile for the photograph but those words were still ringing in my ears as I drove home. Some of those children never knew their parents

November 9th 2002 saw the second year of the Walthamstow Gala Night. Wish Upon a Star was to be the recipient once again. All tickets had been sold a month before the event and some of the items donated as raffle prizes and for the auction, were absolutely wonderful. David remembers that evening well because as I was in the middle of auctioning a tiny teddy bear that I had bought in Woolworths for £2.00. He motioned to a waiter to take his drinks order. I couldn't resist it and closed the deal....sold to brother David for £24.00. The look on his face got the biggest laugh of the night.

2003 started well when in February I was declared William Hill Employee of the Year second year running! 'More luvely jubbly, Rodney.'

On the 17th March I presented 20 Enuresis alarms for young children at St Pancras hospital. I know that incontinence in adults has been the butt of many a comedian's jokes, but when illness induces it in a ten year old, it is very upsetting.

On 1st of November 2003 I commenced the third Walthamstow Gala with the announcement that the money on the night was going to the Whipps X Hospital specialist nursing team. They deliver home help for serious and terminally ill children. It proved to be a very popular decision and all future events right up to the 7th and final one in 2008 were in aid of that wonderful group of people.

Now for anyone sitting there doing their sums, I would quickly add that I was unable to do a Walthamstow Gala night in 2004 due to my cancer, which ironically started out in the waiting area of Whipps X Hospital.

The seventh and final Walthamstow Gala night was bought forward to the 12th July 2008. The stadium was being demolished to make way for a new housing estate. The evening was a sell out and a majority of those attending had been to every event since its inauguration in 2001. The amount raised on the night was over thirteen thousand pounds. Just for the record, the final Arsenal shirt which had been creeping up in price each year, went for £560.

The last ever greyhound race meeting at Walthamstow Stadium took place on 16th August 2008. Jackie and I were invited as guests of the owners, to a private function in the Goodwood Rooms. I sponsored the 11th race and it transpired that Jackie and I did the last ever presentation to the owners and trainer of a winning dog at Walthamstow Stadium! As the 12th and final race was finishing, the exuberant crowd rushed onto the racetrack and parade area and stood there singing and chanting. The officials had no choice but to cancel the race presentation.

In January of that year, I had, at the request of my bosses, entertained 20 dignitaries from Madrid in the function room at Walthamstow Stadium. Now I know what you're thinking but you are wrong. There was never any likelihood of turning the Walthamstow Stadium into a bullfighting arena. The visitors were there as guests of William Hill, to celebrate the company's new venture into Spain. My instructions were 'make them feel at home.' Actually, I think I handled it very well. I based the celebrations on a recent holiday in Magaluf. I put on a little spread of mainly Sangria and olives with pizza and garlic bread. We greeted them with the 'Dickie Bird' song.....Oh yes, and a kiss me quick hat for everyone! At three o'clock in the morning I had them staggering backwards and forwards across Chingford Mount Rd with their shirts off, pissed as farts, singing at the tops of their voices and shouting abuse at passing motorists, followed by a confrontation with the local police. They each took home a plastic greyhound stamped *I Love England*.

In September, I asked Chris Page, who was now the manager at Harlow Greyhound track, If I could work there on my days off from William Hill. I had a scheme in mind that I thought would work well with dog racing. Over the next few weeks, I spoke to several organisations about bringing a minimum thirty plus people to a greyhound race meeting. That would be their team. Six teams were needed on the night and each team could have as many members as they liked. Each team would have a trap number. At the end of the night, the team with the most points won £250. All team challenge members got in for free plus free burger and chips and a free programme. If a club brought one hundred members and charged them a fiver each for the night, that was five hundred quid in the kitty for a start. plus a possible £250 if they won.   Team Challenge had arrived! Eventually, Chris and I formed Team Promotions Ltd and set ourselves up as event organisers. I was able to incorporate Team Challenge into my list of suggestions when asked by various organisations, 'how can we raise money for a worthy cause?' Another good aspect of Team Challenge was that I didn't have to go chasing all over the globe to carry it out personally. I would have a co-ordinator at each participating venue. We would simply send them the tickets and scorecards. The participating club teams could not lose money, on the contrary.

Early in 2009 I brought   shares in a racehorse named Bagsy. The theory was that all prize money would go to cancer charity. Bagsy was based at Julia Fielden's racing stables in Newmarket. What a smashing lady she is. Julia knew all about the cancer charity quest and did us a blinding deal at a fraction of the normal cost. Bagsy turned out to be a beautiful animal and had his first run at Kempton on 21st September. A Sky Sports commentator collared me in the owners' ring and asked a couple of questions about the horse and the unusual charity arrangement us owners had agreed to. Then he turned and said, 'what's does it feel like to be a racehorse owner, Barry?' I had a quick glance around me and replied. 'I've got Sir Michael Stout standing about three feet to my left, Frankie Dettori three feet to my right and the sun is shining. Even if my horse falls asleep in the starting stalls, I'm still having the time of my life!'

Also on duty that night for Channel 4 Racing was Tommo. He knew all about Bagsy and gave him a great build up. Sadly, the horse finished fifth. After a further five races out of the frame, we were beginning to realise that we had a wonderful pet horse but unfortunately, 'not an easy one to back'! That's why none of us were on it when it was switched to hurdles and decided to romp home at 33/1 ..... Story of my life or what?

Unfortunately, that was a one off and we eventually faced up to reality. We were worried about what would happen to the horse if we sold it, so Julia, being the lovely lady that she is, found Bagsy a place in a local riding school. That's where he is today and I daresay the children are spoiling him something rotten.

Fortunately, Team Promotions was doing quite well and other tracks were asking about team challenge events. On 5th February 2010 I organised an event at Crayford dog stadium. Thanks to my team challenge invitation, over 400 **extra** people turned up to take part. The event was a major success, with the public enjoying something different and the track being over four thousand pounds up on its normal takings.

I drove home from Crayford feeling on top of the world, thanks to a conversation that I'd had with a young couple. They had bought their two young children aged 9 and 7 years old and had a great time. I always knew that if I could show 'Joe Public', that dog racing could be fun for **all** the family it would lead to many other possibilities. The man and his wife were full of praise for the fact that they and their children had been able to be part of the team challenge event which had raised over four hundred pounds for their social club funds. The guy summed it all up when he said, 'I always thought that dog racing was all about loads of drunken bone heads shouting, 'gormason' and 'getinthere,' but all we've heard is laughter and praise from people like us who have found something different, something new in life.

Come October, I would start booking clubs in for Team Challenge the following year. I was doubling the gates on a summer's night at some venues. Needless to say, there has been a lot of local interest in Team Challenge on my new track at Towcester. If you're looking for a good night out and a bit of fun with some friends, Team Challenge is for you. The beauty of it is that you don't have to do a thing! You will be part of a team and will have a dog running for you in every race. You just observe your fortunes unfolding as the races are run.

Towcester Park has long been a high quality prestige venue. Not only for horse racing but for society weddings and corporate events. The standard of cuisine in the restaurant is excellent and high rolling punters have access to top champagne at £200 a bottle if they want to push the boat out. But Towcester is going through a transitional period based on preserving the high standards that people have come to expect of them **and** blending in an attractive proposition for family entertainment. The greyhound racing venture has proved very popular, especially on a sunny Sunday when lots of families come. At every meeting the 6th race is dedicated to the children. They are encouraged to gather in the presentation area after that race to have their photo taken with the winning greyhound. Next year I would like to see a monthly 'Family Day', incorporating a large bouncy castle, special rides and a BBQ. We have a Mascot called 'Gracie' at Towcester, the children love having their picture taken with it. Many other ideas are being explored to keep the children entertained and helping to make Towcester Park the best family venue in the county.

Chapter twenty two: Adding it all up

So we arrive at the twilight of my life and career and I pray that the sun will shine for a little longer. The changes over the past two or three years have been massive and I have been through every emotion in the book. This was mostly due to my marriage to Jackie petering out to a point where we both realised that there was no point in carrying on. An arbiter would have reported it as being a total shambles. I was married to my job and my fund raising projects. Jackie was welded to her laptop day and night and would only resort to communication with humans as a last resort. If told that the house was on fire, without looking up, she would settle for, 'get a bucket of water' and would only move her arse if the flames were lapping up around her chair! Even then she would just move to another chair and say, 'get another bucket of water! She was never the happiest person in the world to come home to. How many women do you know that would respond to their husband coming home from work and reporting that he'd been robbed; that he'd had a gun or knife held at their throat and been punched in the ribs, with, 'what do you expect me to do about it?' How about when I'd suffered my tenth armed robbery and was sent for assessment by William Hill, to a Harley Street specialist? I had developed an involuntary shake, was totally stressed out and could not sleep at night. The psychiatric report recommended three months' complete rest to which William Hill agreed. I was totally drained and could probably have slept for a week.

Upon telling my wife the news, her immediate response was, 'I don't want you hanging around the house all day!' Whatever happened to compassion, love and understanding? We had nothing in common anymore. On the contrary, she looked upon me as an intrusion in her life and I rather suspect that it was not 'convenient' for me to be around. Eventually, I took the hint and on Friday 13th July 2012 I moved in with my niece Deborah and her husband Paul. They were fantastic and suddenly, coming home from work took on a whole new meaning. I would walk in to a nice warm welcome, a cooked dinner and a glass of red wine.....or two. Good conversation and occasionally watch the football with Paul. I became aware of how civilised and sane life could be and wished I'd moved out years ago.

After all, the children were grown up and following their chosen careers. Jackie's daughter Angela, who had been half way through studying law at university, had suddenly turned up on the doorstep and announced that she wasn't going back. No idea what happened there. I got her a job with William Hill and she is now managing her own shop. The last I heard was that she was living back home with her mother.

Jackie's son William started out as a shop assistant and is now doing well in retail management. He left home to build a nest with his long term girlfriend, but that didn't work out so they split up. William met someone else and they had a baby! I'm not sure where he is living these days.

My son, George, became a plumber with a local building company and is courting strong. As far as I am aware, he still lives at home with his mum.

The reason I am a bit vague as to where everyone lives at present is because sadly, none of them are talking to me at this moment in time. After a few months' separation, I had the audacity to suggest to Jackie that I should have a share of the property that I had been paying towards for the best part of 24 years. I gave her a figure that everyone considered to be very generous on my part. Her response was both abrasive and unprintable. She dragged it through the courts for two years, courtesy of several expensive adjournments. Not only was it very stressful, as my solicitor commented, it was totally unnecessary.

Finally and thankfully, the courts bought it all to a conclusion and I got my money. During the summing up, the court expressed dissatisfaction at the time wasting due to adjournments. They ordered each party to pay its own costs. I can only imagine that this must have been immense on her part. The court was totally unimpressed with her original offers and awarded me almost double the figure that I had first requested two years earlier. Shooting oneself in the foot springs to mind! It's great to be British sometimes isn't it?

As you can imagine, the whole episode was extremely distressing for me. I was already feeling the strain of the shop robberies over the years and the increase in daily newspaper reports on shop violence was playing on my mind. I was developing a sense of inevitability that I was destined to become a statistic on Crimewatch UK.

'Police are appealing for witnesses after a bullet riddled bookie staggered into a pharmacy in Chingford Hatch asking for a bottle of TCP and some plasters. A barman from a nearby public house was in the pharmacy at the time. As he cradled the leaking bookie in his arms, he noticed that he was trying to say something. He leaned his head forward to listen as the bookie whispered, 'pint of Stella and a packet of crisps please.'

William Hill were extremely understanding in all matters appertaining to my increased anxiety and they realized that I had seen one gun too many. At one point I held the company record of twelve hold ups, but there was no trophy for it. Eventually, they decided to retire me. Sadly, the job did not include a pension but I did receive a generous golden handshake for services rendered. They are a great company to work for and if I had the chance, I would do it all over again.

I would like to make it quite clear that the sort of incidents that I have referred to are happening in shops of all descriptions day after day, all over the country. Anybody who has ever looked down a gun barrel being pointed at them by a drug crazed, bone headed, muscle brained moron, will understand why I believe they should get ten years for just carrying the weapon.

Gambling is a habit, just like smoking, drinking, sex, eating chocolate, burgers and chips and so on. Keep it under control, a once in a while treat can be an enjoyable pleasure. But if you lose control and let it become an addiction, it can ruin your health and bring misery to those around you.

If you lose self respect, how can you expect others to respect you? I love a flutter and have enjoyed being in the betting game for almost 43 years, but when I see a man put his week's wages in a casino machine on a Friday night, I watch him with a feeling of despair and think to myself, 'how can you do that'. By the same token, I love the occasional burger and chips or a pizza. But when I see a twenty two stone dollop of fat walking down the road towards me, I shake my head and think, how can you do that to yourself?

You can either have self control or be controlled. The feeling of adrenalin when your horse surges towards the winning post is magical. So is picking up £80 for a fiver each way. But if you start out with a couple of losers, walk away and live to fight another day. Never chase lost money!

A night out at the dogs is great, especially if there's a few of you having a laugh. If you bet two pounds on each race, you would have to be extremely unlucky not to have at least two or three pickups during the twelve race evening. But even if the worst comes to the worst, the most you will lose is twenty four pounds.

Whether it be a night at the dogs, horse racing or in a casino, put your betting money (the most you can afford to lose) in a separate pocket. Bet from that pocket and spread the money over a few races. If you double your *pocket money* in the first few races, take out the amount you started with and forget about it! Play on with your winnings for the rest of the evening. Now you can't lose. However, if you empty your pocket in the first few races, walk away. Remember, that's the most you can afford to lose and there's always next time.

Looking around a top betting shop these days is almost like being in a space ship. But I can still remember the first year that TV screens were allowed in betting shops. It was 1986 and it drew the crowds in like a magnet.

TV coverage was nowhere near as comprehensive as nowadays, but it was a chance to see your horse run. Betting shop managers absolutely loved this new concept because it gave them the chance to get to know their punters. Some would even put the kettle on and enjoy a smoke and a chat. Not everyone lived two minutes round the corner to their local betting shop. So, having watched their horse run, most would stay for a while and have a few more bets. Within weeks some shops had doubled their turnover.

Almost ten years later, on the 7th May 1995 to be precise, another landmark in racing occurred. Despite massive opposition from the church authorities, thanks to new legislation, the government agreed to a trial run of allowing betting shops to open on a Sunday. Eleven days that year and eventually, every Sunday, the only sacred day left was Good Friday.

Betting shops were now becoming very popular as meeting places and many managers put out a few snacks and cups of tea to keep their regulars happy. In 2001 a few shops incorporated the newest innovation in gambling. FOBT machines. Or Fixed Odds Betting Terminal, to give its full name.

Starting out as glorified 'fruit machines' their popularity grew like wildfire along with their sophistication. Today, if you live in a town or a city, you will not be too far away from your own mini casino. FOBT machines have become the biggest money spinners in the history of gambling. Ironically, they have secured the future of betting shops.

Another big change occurred in the betting industry in 2005. It was the year that the EPOS machines were installed. Electronic Point Of Sale technology meant that a machine could calculate and settle a bet in seconds. A process that I and so many of my older colleagues had persevered to perfect with a pen and pad was now possible at press of a button. All the formulas and short cuts that we had carried in our heads for thirty years were now obsolete. I've lost count of the number of times I was able to impress a group of friends with my favourite party piece. That's it! My social life in ruins thanks to some Japanese smart arse with a degree in electronics...thank you so much...you bastard!

I can't remember the exact month, but back in 2007, some fucking insomniac decided that betting shops could stay open until 10pm seven nights a week. This was the kiss of death for my nervous system. I was being mugged, robbed and threatened in broad daylight but now the assailants also had cover of darkness on their side. I was so on edge at times, it was all I could do when the shop door opened, to stop myself from diving on the floor screaming, 'don't shoot!'

David walked into my Hatch Lane shop one day, carrying a large parcel under his arm. He knew of my growing concern about being alone in the shop at ten o'clock at night. As I put his mug of coffee on the counter, I looked at the giant package which must have been about four foot square, and said, 'what have you got there?. He looked at me and said, 'where?' I said, 'under your arm you silly sod....what is it?' He looked down all nonchalantly and said, 'oh that? It's just something I knocked up to help prevent you from being lonely...you can hang it outside the shop.' I watched as he unwrapped the brown paper and held up a board. It read, FREE TEA AND SANDWICHES FOR ALL POLICE OFFICERS. I laughed as I put it behind the counter. He should have been on television that one.

Oh! And for anybody out there who thinks that us betting shop managers were raking it in with all this overtime, don't even go there! We were given extra time off to make up for working late. Imagine me going into Tesco's and reaching the tills to be told, 'that's £8.55 please, and I jokingly reply, 'can I pay you in time off?' We accumulated 'time off' by working late, then you would get days off in recognition. Sometimes I would do six days on and get four days off. That would have been more palatable if I'd lived with normal people. But to sit staring at Mrs Sourface for four days, whilst enduring comments such as, 'what you doing at home?' I found myself praying for a stick up, to bring a bit of excitement into my life. At least it would have served to further my ever growing awareness of how many different types of hand gun there were in circulation..

On the 21st of March 2008, the last bastion of decency was removed from our long, illustrious heritage. Betting shops were allowed to open on Good Friday. There was no racing on mind you, but the machines were raking in so much money, it didn't matter......cuh! More time off!

Over the years, I've watched punters pumping thousands of pounds into Casino machines not knowing when to quit. Sometimes it's the booze and other times it's just plain bloody mindedness. As they kick the machine and walk out moaning, I can't help thinking of all the good that money would have done for sick children. Now, my bosses at William Hill were always brilliant when it came to my fund raising exploits but they would quite rightly argue that people were in the shop trying to win money from us whilst we were trying to win money off them. Don't get me wrong, I've seen some folk walk out of my shops with their pockets bulging. Knowing when to quit before you give it all back, that's the secret.

I was looking through my office drawer and came across some papers relating to a series of fund raising projects that I did for Waltham Forest NHS a few years ago. Just a small example of one of many such projects that I was able to carry out in my spare time. You'll notice that I was inactive during 2004. That's the year I had my cancer operations and treatment. The NHS at Barts was superb and I thank them for looking after me. Payback time you could say!

The National Health Service is always short of essential equipment. Government funding is never enough. This is part of a document that they posted in one of their finance reports.

Waltham Forest NHS Primary Care Trust. Specialist Children's Service

Equipment purchased from fund raising monies, the majority of which has been raised by Barry Coombs from the William Hill organisation

In addition to the following list, we have been able to provide occasional presents for many of the children known to specialist children's services to have chronic or life limiting illness and varying degrees of

disability. Just a small gift to help them celebrate their special day.

Our special thanks to Barry and his team.

PURCHASES FROM FUNDRAISING MONIES

DATE	EQUIPMENT	COST	TEAM
January 2004	IVAC P6000 Syringe Driver	£1696.00	CCNT
February 2005	Datex Ohmeda Sats Monitor	£1290.00	CCNT
March 2005	Pari Uni Light Mobil Nebuliser	£243.00	CCNT
April 2005	Pari Uni Light Mobil Nebuliser	£243.00	CCNT
May 2005	3 Repose Pressure Relieving Mattress/cushion/pumps	£302	CCNT
April 2006	Datex Ohmeda Sats Monitor	£1290	CCNT
April 2006	3 Pari E Flow Rapid Nebulisers 3 Aerosel heads & 3 mouthpieces	£1390	CCNT
April 2006	2 Repose Pressure Relieving Mattress Sets	£198.00	CCNT
April 2006	10 Enuresis Alarms	£450.00	SCHOOL NURSES
May 2006	1 Glideaway Parents Bed	£498.00	ACORN CHILDREN'S UNIT
September 2006	2 Laerdal Suction Units	£1250.00	CCNT
September 2006	2 Infant Ambu Bags	£20.00	CCNT
December 2006	2 Laerdal Suction Bags 2 Shoulder Straps	£39.00	CCNT
December 2006	1 Laerdal Suction Unit	£625.00	CCNT
January 2007	15 Enuresis Alarms	£675.00	SCHOOL NURSING
January 2007	1 Glideaway Parents Bed	£519.75	ACORN CHILDREN'S UNIT
January 2007	Battery for BP Machine, BP Machine 1 carry bag	£1109.95	CCNT
March 2007	2 Pari E Flow Rapid Nebulisers	£850.00	CCNT

The Waltham Forest document shown is just a small example of the work carried out by voluntary fund raising groups up and down the country. As you can see, this is essential medical equipment and furniture which has not been affordable from the annual budget allowance granted by the government. Although I have not enclosed all the pages on this report, the total amount on this inventory alone was £33,646.37. All paid for by voluntary fund raising. There were many similar projects that I was involved in over the years.

I think that it is deplorable for the government of this country to pour billions of pounds each year into benefits for thousands of people who are quite capable of going to work but are too bloody lazy. Much of the benefit money handed out to these people goes on drugs and alcohol, cars and even holidays abroad! Yet the government, to its eternal shame, is quite happy to sit back and let private fund raising ventures come to the rescue of an over loaded and underpaid group of people, any one of which is worth a hundred benefit cheats.

Recent changes in my lifestyle and location have temporarily restricted my fund raising activities. Self indulgence has also played a major part. Two and a half years ago I met a very special lady named Wing. We have become soul mates and love each other to the moon and back. My family and friends can see that Wing is good for me and they love her as well. We are house hunting at the moment, but as soon as we have settled down Barry the Charity will be back in circulation. So spend it while you can people, because I'll be out to confirm that you can't take it with you and that there are many who need it more than you.

There is still much to do and I pray that I will have the strength to do it for a few more years to come. At the last conservative estimate, my fund raising activities have amounted to around half a million pounds for sick children. It has been an absolute privilege to be in a position to help these youngsters. Also, I am so proud to live in a society that cares and to be part of a nation that takes pride and sets the standards in helping desperate people all around the world. There but for fortune!

THE END

Barry Coombs

A Special Thanks

I would like to say a special thank you to some of the people who have influenced and encouraged me along the way: my childhood was full of love and happiness. I think of my loving parents constantly. My teenage years were crazy but harmless. In particular, I remember with affection my fellow ghost hunters, Ian Carden, Dave Lister and Eion Tomkins, who is now head of religious studies at Maidstone Grammar School.

A big thank you to my friends and colleagues at William Hill; for encouraging and supporting me both mentally and financially in my constant crusade to raise funds for an endless list of worthy causes. C.E.O. James Henderson booked three tables for the WH staff every year at the Walthamstow Gala. Also, Martyn Pearce and his team deserve a big thank you.

If David Colane is looking for another story, he should talk to my dear friends Chris Page, Mick Davis and 'technician extraordinaire' Lee Kinkaid. Definitely enough memories there for a best seller. Just set the beers up, find a comfortable chair, take the phone off the hook, sit back and listen.

If I were to choose one person who has changed and influenced my life the most, it would have to be John 'Curly' Wilson. It was John who opened my eyes to the harsh reality of children suffering from serious illness, as a result of which, I came to experience the overwhelming sense of satisfaction and achievement felt when helping to brighten up their lives. God bless you John.

I am so fortunate to be surrounded by love. My beautiful partner Wing, is the most patient, understanding and loving person I have ever come across. Ben and Chantelle my children from the first marriage have given me five beautiful grandchildren, Callum, Courtney, Holly, Taylah and baby Liam. Love them all to bits.

My brother David and his partner, the author Jan Mount, live in a beautiful house out in the countryside. He is still my favourite comedian and we were both blessed with our parent's great sense of humour and love for our fellow man....and woman! I think the song 'Always Look On The Bright Side Of Life' might have been written with him in mind.

Finally, I would like to thank the author David Colane of Penskills Publishing, for writing my story. When I began dictating periods of my career and fund raising exploits to him, he was intending to produce a simple straight forward autobiography. But as I related various aspects of my outrageous childhood and private life, he suddenly insisted that my story should be told to a much larger audience. He changed the format and apparently the 'bookshelf' and finally wrote a novel based on the life and times of Barry The Charity/Bookie/Bastard/whatever? His skills with the pen have enabled me to look back on events and to laugh at them all over again.

It has dawned on me that as soon as we left school, my brothers and I should have been forced to either join a monastery or attend a course on the pitfalls of marriage. Not one successful first marriage between us.

Donald was divorced once whilst David and I had two disastrous attempts, each one ending in shambles. I believe that lessons in our early teens would have taught us the real qualities to look for in a lifelong partner to be. Thankfully, albeit a bit late in life, David and I have found our perfect soul mates. Dave and Jan in their country retreat, sloping off to Malta when the fancy takes them and enjoying their social circle. Whilst I, being in the prime of life have found total love and contentment with Wing Man.

Wing and I love London and the seaside. We have an excursion to somewhere special once a week and leave all our cares behind us. She is the perfect partner for me and accepts me for what I am. (whatever that is?)

Since being with Wing, I have put on over a stone in weight. Thankfully, my three days a week at Towcester entails much walking around and several trips up and down the stairs to the private suites etc. Come and see me on a Friday, Saturday or Sunday when the greyhound meetings are on at Towcester Park. It's a great experience for all the family and you can get your book signed by me.

Barry Coombs

A few special words

I would like to tell you about a very special girl called Carol. My mother and father had four sons. Lawrence, Donald, David and me. Lawrence was killed in a road accident before I was born. My parents' grief was immense and all consuming. There was also anger and bitterness over the way he died. As devout Christians my parents wanted to replace this bitterness with love. They adopted a newborn baby girl and called her Carol. Once more our house could hear the sound of laughter.

Sadly, tragedy struck again when, at the age of three, Carol caught poliomyelitis, leaving her mentally retarded and in leg irons. Over the next ten years, whilst attending specialist centres and learning to walk and talk again, Carol developed epilepsy. At sixteen years old with the mental age of five and a terrible stutter, Carol's frustration caused her mood swings to be dangerously unpredictable with outburst of violence. Sadly, she spent the rest of her life in special care residence.

Carol was receiving the best possible care and attention. As we watched other people visiting seriously ill members of their family, I became aware of the constant pressure and sadness they were experiencing. Carol passed away aged sixty four. It would take another book to tell her story in full. Whenever I get involved in raising funds to help a sick child, I think of my sister, Carol. May her soul rest in eternal peace.